W9-DEX-008

the
pagan book
of days

the
paGan
book
of
Days

A Guide to the
Festivals, Traditions,
and Sacred Days
of the Year

Nigel Pennick

Destiny Books
Rochester, Vermont

Destiny Books
One Park Street
Rochester, Vermont 05767
www.InnerTraditions.com

Destiny Books is a division of Inner Traditions International

Library of Congress Cataloging-in-Publication Data

Pennick, Nigel.
    The pagan book of days : a guide to the festivals, traditions, and sacred
days of the year / Nigel Pennick.
        p. cm.
    Includes index.
    ISBN 0-89281-369-5
    1. Religious calendars. 2. Seasons—Religious aspects.   3. Rites and
ceremonies. 4. Festivals. 5. Paganism—rituals I. Title
BL 590.P45 1992
291.3'6—dc20   92–10338
                                          CIP

Printed and bound in the United States

10 9 8 7

Text design and layout by Virginia L. Scott-Bowman

contents

Introduction

T HE PAGAN TRADITION is grounded in mystical and numinous elements existing between matter and spirit. The world over it is called something like "the old religion," or "the elder faith," acknowledging its senior status among religions. It places emphasis on the links between people, their land, and the natural cycles of the seasons. In industrialized countries this connection is almost lost, because many people no longer feel rooted in the soil or connected to the seasons. In contrast, Pagan myth and ritual embody a profound respect for the physical world and the seasonal nature of the sacred year. In the Pagan sacramental vision, to live according to the natural year is to be in harmony with all things natural and supernatural.

The elder faith is based on the joyful celebration of life itself. An awareness of the natural year observed through seasonal rites and ceremonies brings a positive attitude to all processes and stages of life. As the years pass and each festival is celebrated again, new meanings and insights come into focus. One of the most important elements of Paganism is its respect for the goddess and the feminine principle. The elder faith accepts it as self-evident that, for there to be balance, the female and the male must complement each other.

Worship of the goddess as Isis, Shakti, Kuan-yin, Aphrodite, Freya, Selene, and in other forms takes place in Egyptian, Hindu, Taoist, Greek, Norse, Roman, and Native American religions, as well as in moon worship. It provides a balance with patriarchal forms of worship such as Druidism, which are essentially solar-based paths.

The worship of the goddesses and gods of northern Europe, in their varied aspects, is known as the Northern, and sometimes Western, Pagan Tradition. This includes the Norse, Anglo-Saxon, and Frisian deities, as well as those of the Celtic and Baltic pantheons. The worship of the Norse deities is known as Asatru (faith in the divinities collectively known as the Aesir). In Odinism, and part of the Teutonic tradition, the Norse god Odin (the Anglo-Saxon Woden, or Wotan) is the chief divinity. Other aspects of Paganism are present in the American tradition. The initiated mystery tradition of Paganism is mostly known as Wicca, or Wicce, with a root meaning of forming or using nature according to the skills of its adepts.

The Pagan Book of Days lists sacred days of the natural year from the above traditions—the Anglo-Saxon, Norse, Celtic, and Northern traditions—as well as some from Pagan Greece and Rome. The country calendar used here is from the tradition of my part of England, East Anglia (the counties of Norfolk, Suffolk, Cambridgeshire, and parts of Essex). It was the last place where the mystic Society of the Horseman's Word existed (until 1950). The rural tradition of "cunning men" and "wise women" (the tradition with no name) has continuity here. I am part of it. Traditional deities, saints' days, weather lore, and customs are from this calendar. More details about this tradition can be found in my book *Practical Magic in the Northern Tradition* (Aquarian, 1989).

Real Time

All of the world's religious traditions teach that sacred rites and observances should be performed not only on the correct day but also at the correct time. Unfortunately, this is not as easy as it might first appear. Time systems are often related to national or supranational areas and are only precise along their meridian of origin. If we casually use local clock time for our ceremonies, then the chances are that it will have only a remote connection with solar time, or *real time*. Standard times, arranged in zones from which our clock time is taken, rarely correspond with true solar local time. For example, the west of Ireland and London are in the same time zone but the sun rises later and sets later in Galway than in Cambridge. Likewise in the United States, both Boston and western Michigan are in the same time zone but a mid-August sunset will be a full hour later in western Michigan than eastern Massachusetts.

In order to harmonize correctly with the natural cycles of heaven, all times used in sacred observances should be defined in real time, that is, time determined by the actual visible position of the sun at the appropriate place on the earth's surface. Because we are on the surface of a rotating planet, when we tell the time by the sun we are noting its apparent location in relation to our position. This is known as local apparent time (LAT) or real time, and it is the time that is shown by a sundial where the shadow points to the time on the dial. Midday or high noon is taken as the point of reference and is defined as the time when the sun is due south.

At any one time, a person at any point on a given meridian will see the sun in the same direction. A meridian is an imaginary line that runs from the north pole to the south pole. When the sun is due south in relation to the meridian, the time at any place along it is noon. Places located to the east of the meridian are in the afternoon, and to its west in the forenoon. A place 15° of longitude to the east or west will be one hour in front or behind, respectively, of any corresponding meridian. Even a seemingly minor distance to the east or west of a meridian makes a significant time difference. Also, the nearer one gets to the poles, then the shorter the distance between meridians becomes. The east-west distance which makes a time difference of one second is 1075 feet (328 meters) at the latitude of 45° and 872 feet (266 meters) at the latitude of 55°. The time-zone method of defining time takes the mean time at a given longitude, such as the Greenwich meridian, and establishes it as being the time over a zone that might extend as far as 7° to 30° of longitude to either side of the meridian. Because of this, places near the boundaries of the zone have a standard time that has little connection with real time at that place.

Political boundaries and other factors in some places add up to two hours' deviation from actual solar time, and in some countries an hour is added on in summertime. This can have the effect of making real time solar noon, that is, when the sun stands due south, the best part of three hours after noon by the clock. Clearly, at such times, any natural sacred observance that uses clock time will be far away from true solar time. To calculate real time in any place, find the time at the nearest time-zone meridian and then determine the difference in longitude of the place from the meridian. For each degree west deduct four minutes from meridian time, and add four minutes if east. Yearly almanacs often list the longitude and latitude of cities throughout the country and also provide formulas for adjusting standard time to local or real time. For precise astrological times consult a standard ephemeris, and then make the appropriate adjustments.

Another aspect of clock time is the unnatural regularity that it keeps. Clocks are mechanical or electronic machines that depend on mechanisms operating at a precise, constant rate. But Mother Earth is not a machine. When measured by the sun at different times of the year, days vary in length because the earth rotates at variable speeds depending on its proximity to or distance from the sun as it moves in its elliptical orbit. Because of this irregularity, official time is reckoned from a hypothetically accurate sun that moves at a constant speed, creating an average day of twenty-four regular hours. In reality, the sun sometimes runs ahead of and at other times behind this average mean time. Around St. Oswy's Day, 15 February, the sun stands on the meridional line—local noon—nearly fourteen minutes later than noon as meaured by clock time. Around Samhain, 1 November, local noon takes place sixteen minutes earlier than noon as measured by clock time. Only on 16 April (St. Padarn's), 14 June (St. Dogmael's), 2 September (St. Sulien's), and 25 December does real time coincide with mean time.

An awareness of real time in sacred observances can bring us into harmony with nature and the inherent natural qualities of time.

The Calendar

All calendars are human attempts to define the essentially indefinable continuous flow of time, and, as such, all are to some extent arbitrary. In Europe and equally in North America, the year is divided naturally by the seasons, which are easily perceived. But there were once perceptions of lesser divisions, marked by the days annually given to deities possessing qualities corresponding with the time of year. In the Western tradition the perceived influences of the sun, moon, and planets are identified with deities, and the names of weekdays are a reflection of this. Rituals marked all these special days and influences as a way of aligning our lives with the cycles permeating all life on Earth.

The Tides of the Day

The most obvious cycle of all is that of day and night. Conventionally, the day is divided into twenty-four equal hours, based upon a day beginning at midnight (00:00 hours). During the daylight hours the position of the sun is easily determined with regard to the horizon. Each moment of daytime equals a specific sun direction. Similarly, at night, although invisible, the sun is in a specific direction. The twenty-four-hour day, as defined by a complete solar cycle, can be divided into eight groups of three hours each. In the Northern Tradition these are known as the eight tides of the day, called *airts* or *aettir*. The tides are a practical way of marking time, and it should be noted that they bear no relationship to the tides of the ocean, whose cycles are influenced mainly by the gravitational effects of the moon. Each of the tides of the day is related to one of the eight directions of the compass rose and its corresponding wind. They are not actual directions of course, and each one symbolizes a specific esoteric quality. The midpoint of each tide is called the *aetting*. It is at that time that the corresponding quality or virtue is at its most effective. For example, the aetting of midnight, 00:00 hours, is at the middle of the tide of midnight

and corresponds with the north and the north wind, Septentrio. Each
aetting is a special time of day. People born at these times, known as the
chime hours (midnight, 3 A.M., 6 A.M., 9 A.M., noon, 3 P.M., 6 P.M., and 9 P.M.), are
said to have second sight and the power to foretell the future and see
supernatural beings. The tides of the day and their corresponding winds,
directions, and virtues can be seen in the following table.

The Tides of Day

TIME	OLD WELSH	MODERN	WIND	DIRECTION	VIRTUE
04:30–07:30	Bore	Morntide	Solanus	East	Arousal Awakening Fertility Vitality
07:30–10:30	Anterth	Undernoon	Eurus	Southeast	Gentleness Earning Gain, money
10:30–13:30	Nawn	Noontide	Auster	South	Sustenance
13:30–16:30	Echwydd	Undorne	Africus	Southwest	Receptivity
16:30–19:30	Gwechwydd	Eventide	Favonius	West	Parenting Joyousness Spirit Family Children
19:30–22:30	Ucher	Nighttide	Cautus	Northwest	Creativity Teaching
22:30–01:30	Dewaint	Midnight	Septentrio	North	Stasis Healing Regeneration
01:30–04:30	Pylgaint	Uht	Aquilo	Northeast	Stillness Sleep Death

Traditional Days

The word *day* has more than one meaning. Most commonly, it refers to
the official period of twenty-four hours associated with a calendar date,

each day beginning at midnight. But this is not the traditional definition of a day. In ancient Greece, for example, the day was reckoned to run from dawn until the following dawn. The day in the central and northern European tradition begins at sunset, as it does in the Jewish tradition. Symbolically and literally, this day starts in darkness and continues through the next period of daylight until the following sunset. This is why all of the customary festivals of the year are preceded by an eve or aften, taken as being the night before. Even in secular usage they are still common: New Year's Eve, May Eve, All Hallows' Eve (Halloween), and Christmas Eve, to name but a few. Sometimes, however, the word *eve* is applied erroneously to the whole calendar day.

The universal use of calendar dates has caused confusion, making the evening before the festival appear to be separate. In the natural year, the first part of any festival day is its eve, a prelude to the daylight festivities or observances held on the morrow. The gestation of the festive day takes place in the darkness that comes before the daylight.

Egyptian Days

The natural year recognizes the cyclic nature of time. Equally, it recognizes that good times are followed by bad times, and bad times in turn by good times. Because each day of the year is a part of many cycles, so certain days are traditionally considered to be bringers of good or bad fortune. Traditional calendar lore cites a number of inauspicious days upon which it is considered inadvisable to commence any undertaking. At one time, they were days upon which it was considered hazardous if one should fall ill, commence a work project, start a journey, or be married. Fridays with

the date 13 were widely believed to be such days, yet there are others whose inauspiciousness does not relate to the day of the week upon which they fall. These, derived ultimately from Alexandrian year lore, are known as Egyptian Days (Dies Aegyptiacae). Clearly, it is not necessary to hold these dates in superstitious terror, preventing all action, but it is wise to take note of them as having been considered inauspicious for over 2300 years.

The Days of the Week

The final means of classifying days is the seven-day cycle that originated in ancient Babylonian astrology, where a continuous repeating sequence of attributes is given to the days, regardless of their calendar date. The days of the week are named after the gods and goddesses who are their rulers. Most of them are Anglo-Saxon in origin. The deities are equivalent to the sun, moon, and five major planets, whose qualities are believed to be especially active on their corresponding days. According to this view, those activities that relate to these qualities are more likely to succeed on the corresponding day.

Traditionally, Sunday is the first day of the week. It is also known as the Lord's Day from its original association with the Lord, that is, the sun god, personified as Helios, Apollo, Ogmios, Mithras, and St. Elias. But in the Northern Tradition, the sun is seen as feminine, personified as the goddess known as Phoebe in East Anglia and Saule in eastern Europe. The sun rules the conscious element of the human being, the ego, the real self, and Sunday is the day on which this conscious power is at its most effective.

Monday is the sacred day of the moon, personified as the goddesses Selene, Luna, and Mani. The moon is ruler of flow, affecting the changeable and impressionable aspects of people. If a full moon falls on a Monday, then the powers of the moon are at their most potent.

Tuesday is dedicated to the powers of the planet Mars, personified as Ares, Tiwaz, Tiw, Tuisco, and Tyr. Tuesday rules controlled power, energy, and endurance.

Wednesday is the day of the Teutonic deity known as Woden or Odin, an aspect of the Allfather, god of knowledge, wisdom, enlightenment, and combat, the parallel of Hermes, the planet Mercury.

Thursday is the day of the planet Jupiter, dedicated to Thunor (Thor), god of thunder and agricultural work. His parallels in various European traditions are Zeus, Taranis, Perun, Perkunas, and St. Olaf. The faith of the Northern Tradition holds Thursday sacred, just as Islam reveres Friday, Judaism the Sabbath (calculated from sunset on Friday to sunset on Saturday), and Christianity, Sunday. This is why almost all adages about Thursday are positive, such as "Thursday's child has far to go," "Sneeze on Thursday, something better," or "Cut nails on Thursday for wealth." Thursday rules controlled optimism, energetic growth, physical well-being, and material success.

Friday is the day of Venus. It takes its name from Frigg, the goddess of love and transformation. She rules the spiritual side of a person that manifests in the physical. Because of this, Friday is often thought of as dangerously unpredictable. This is expressed in an old East Anglian adage:

> *Friday's day will have its trick,*
> *The fairest or foulest day of the week.*

Saturday is dedicated to the shadowy Anglo-Saxon god Saetere or Seater, equivalent to the god Saturn. It is a day also associated with the Norns, the Norse equivalent of Three Fates, and the trickster god Loki. It is connected generally with apprehension, austerity, caution, and excessive self-limitation.

Traditional lore describes these qualities of the days in terms of their effect upon specific events. For example, the day on which a couple is married was once considered important, producing corresponding results:

> *Monday for wealth,*
> *Tuesday for health,*
> *Wednesday, the best day of all,*
> *Thursday for losses,*
> *Friday for crosses,*
> *And Saturday, no luck at all.*

Also, the day on which one was born is said to govern one's fortune and character in life:

> *Monday's child is fair of face,*
> *Tuesday's child is full of grace,*
> *Wednesday's child is full of woe,*
> *Thursday's child has far to go,*
> *Friday's child is loving and giving,*
> *Saturday's child works hard for a living.*
> *But the child that is born on the Sabbath day*
> *Is blithe and bonny, good and gay.*

These rhymes, now generally considered trite, are reminders to the modern age that the qualities of time were once taken seriously. These qualities are based upon the traditional doctrine of correspondences that associates the days not only with divinities but also with elements, sacred trees, herbs, lucky numbers, and runes—the magical alphabet of Germany, Scandinavia, and Britain. The sacred and magical qualities of the runes are more potent on their corresponding day than at other times. The Northern correspondences for the days of the week are as follows:

DAY	DEITY	PLANET	TREE	HERB	ELEMENT	NO.	RUNE
Mon	Mani	Moon	Willow	Chickweed	Water	5	Lagu (L)
Tues	Tiwaz	Mars	Holly	Plantain	Fire	2	Tyr (T)
Wed	Woden	Mercury	Ash	Cinquefoil	Air	6	Odal (O)
Thur	Thor	Jupiter	Oak	Henbane	Fire	3	Thorn (TH)
Fri	Frigg	Venus	Apple	Vervain	Earth	7	Peorth (P)
Sat	Saetere	Saturn	Alder	Daffodil	Earth	4	Dag (D)
Sun	Sol	Sun	Birch	Snakeroot	Fire	1	Sigel (S)

Notable Days

Individual notable days derive their significance in a number of ways. Most of the sacred days of the Pagan and Christian religions—including most of those listed in this book—are fixed, meaning that they are celebrated on the same day every year. New Year's Day, 1 January (the end and beginning of the 365-day solar year), and Beltane, 1 May (the midpoint between the vernal equinox and summer solstice), are two such days. Other sacred days are defined by the Christian saints or their Pagan forerunners—the attributes of both often being the same: thus St. George's slaying of the dragon echoes the killing of the Chimera by Bellerophon, while St. Clement's patronage of smiths continues that of the older godling, Wayland. Frequently, in addition to their attributes, the actual names of the saints are almost identical to those of the earlier deities that they supplanted. St. Januarius is none other than the two-faced Roman god Janus; St. Febronia is the goddess Juno Februa; St. Cecilia, patroness of music, is Artemis Calliste. Although the cult of saints was abolished by the

Protestants at the Reformation, the rural farmer's and hunter's lore continued to observe dual-faith holy days as the essential markers of the annual cycle. Because of this, even in countries where the Protestant churches were dominant, the ancient knowledge and use of these days has continued unbroken into modern times.

Still other sacred or festival days are movable and change every year. The equinoxes and solstices may vary by as much as a day from year to year, but aside from these four solar events, movable feasts are generally derived from the phases of the moon. These movable days are observed today in various Pagan traditions and by the Church in the Easter cycle of festivals. Easter is the most important lunar-derived festival of the Pagan year. This is the lunar spring celebration of the goddess Eostre or Ostara. Technically, Easter should be observed on the first Sunday that occurs after the first full moon following the vernal equinox, providing that this full moon does not occur on 21 March! However, in the present Gregorian calendar, the moon phase used in the calculation is not always the real full moon we can see. Sometimes the calculation is deliberately incorrect. This curious calendar aberration was created with the intention that the celebration of the Christian Easter would never coincide with the Jewish Passover, which is calculated on a similar basis. Later comes Ascension Day, upon which some German Pagan groups celebrate the festival of Mjollnir, Thor's Hammer. After this, Pentecost, or Whitsunday, is the final lunar festival observed by the Church. In modern German Pagan usage, it is called High May. In this book movable feasts appear under the days on which they occur in 1993 and are marked with a small sun ☉ or moon ☽. These refer the reader to the corresponding charts at the back of the book: the sun chart on page 145 for equinoxes and solstices and the moon chart on page 144 give the dates for other movable days from 1993, the base year for the book, through the year 2000.

The Phases of the Moon

The moon's phases have not been included in the month-by-month daybook because the moon does not keep to solar calendar time. The traditional meaning of the moon's phases is not affected by the calendar date

on which they fall; each of the phases symbolizes various aspects of the goddess. (Tables of the moon's phases from 1993 through the year 2000 can be found on pages 146-148.)

The new moon, the dark moon, begins the two waxing quarters of the lunar cycle. Confusingly, however the crescent moon is often called the new moon, too. This second phase is identified with the maiden or virgin. She is described as a young and beautiful woman and is related to the goddess Artemis or Diana. The waxing moon is a time of beginnings and growth. It is traditional to plant herbs when the moon is in the signs of Pisces, Cancer, or Scorpio.

The full moon symbolizes the mother. From beyond the first quarter the moon is seen as the pregnant woman. Her daily growth to roundness brings her to womanhood in full flower, the goddess Selene or Luna. Full moon is a time of power, ripeness, and the honoring of helpers and guides.

The third quarter, or last quarter, is the postmenopausal woman, sometimes pejoratively called the crone. As a goddess, she is the Greek Hecate and the Celtic Morrigan. The waning moon is a time for divination, overcoming obstacles, and relinquishing bad habits or thoughts. Customarily, weeding the garden and ploughing are done during this part of the moon cycle.

In the Anatolian tradition of Wicca, the threefold goddess is divided threefold once more, into nine distinct forms of each moon.

The Goddess Days of the Moon

DAY	GODDESS
Days 1-3	Dedicated to Persephone, the initiator
Days 4-6	Ruled by Artemis, the independent one of the wilderness, the impetus behind the newly planted seed
Days 7-9	Kore rules these lunar days, and she is seen as the Maiden of Menarche, the link between childhood and adulthood
Days 10-12	Ruled by Hera, queen of heaven and creatrix, representing the power of inspiration
Days 13-15	Demeter, the nurturer, is ruler
Days 16-18	Dedicated to Gaia, the earth goddess
Days 19-21	In these days the old woman of the waning moon is Hestia; she is the matriarchal grandmother ruling and protecting her family
Days 22-24	Ruled by Medusa, the terrible crone of death and spiritual release, the necessary destruction that allows a new cycle to begin
Days 25-27	Ruled by Hecate, queen of the underworld and the shades; she is seen as the one who allows departed souls to choose their paths in the next phase of existence and rebirth

The remaining days of the moon—the dark days—are those of the unknowable Masked Goddess who is present, but invisible.

The Festivals of the Natural Year

In central and northern Europe, the natural year is measured by eight major festival days. These days are the equinoxes and solstices of the sun's year and the four cross-quarter days that come between them. They are observed by all followers of nature religions.

Of the eight festivals, four—the equinoxes and solstices—are movable: they are defined by the apparent movement of the sun. The equinoxes are at the center of this movement, and the solstices are the endpoints of the sun's motion. These four solar points represent the mutual relationships inherent in the interaction between light and darkness. They are genuinely cosmic festivals whose timing is dependent upon the dynamics of Earth and Sun. Traditionally, the qualities of these times have been associated with the male aspects of existence, personified as the sky gods. The festival of midwinter, the complex that includes Yule and Christmas, is the clearest instance of this.

The four major remaining festivals of the natural year are recognized as more feminine in their quality. They are the earth-defined festivals, related to the cycle of plant growth and the changes of the seasons. Traditionally, these four cross-quarter days are known as the fire festivals. Each has a fire ceremony whose origin is of great antiquity. They were the most important festivals of the Druids, held on fixed dates in February, May, August, and November.

The eight festivals are as follows:

Imbolc (Oimelc) and Candlemas, celebrated on 1 and 2 February, mark the end of winter and the beginning of spring and celebrate the

waxing light when, although cold, the days are lengthening. Imbolc represents the first stirring of the buried seeds within the earth. Symbolically, it is a time of renewal, cleansing, and rebirth. The day is also called Brigantia, after the virgin goddess Bridhe (Bride or Bridget). On this day, the goddess Bridhe expresses her threefold attributes: the powers of healing, firecraft, and poetry. In Asatru, the branch of the Pagan faith that worships the old Saxon and Norse divinities, she is Birgit, spring-loving consort of Ullr, god of winter. At Imbolc, the threefold goddess is transformed from her winter aspect as the aged hag, veiled in black. She throws aside her black rod of wintry barrenness and is transformed into the radiant virgin bride, springing from seeming death into life.

Under Christian influence, this festival was assimilated into the feast of the Purification of the Virgin, known commonly as Candlemas from the observance of lighting candles at midnight as symbols of purification. In Ireland, the worship of the Virgin at Candlemas is particularized as St. Bridhe's Day, La Fheile Bridhe, celebrating St. Brigid, the continuation of the Pagan Mother goddess in her aspect as the virgin. The goddess's symbol, the asymmetric cross, best known now in the form of St. Bridhe's cross, can be made on Imbolc Eve and put up in the house for protection against fire, lightning, and storm. The traditional sigil of Imbolc is a five-branched stave, signifying the upraised hand with spread fingers. This is a version of the protective Elhaz (Elk) rune. The ceremonial color for the spring quarter of the year, which begins at Imbolc, is red.

Alban Eilir, Ostara, or the vernal equinox, on or about 20 March, is the second festival of the natural year and marks the changeover point between the dark and light halves of the year. At this time, the sun rises due east and sets due west, gives exactly twelve hours of daylight, and begins its increase. Although modern bureaucracy classifies the equinox as the first day of spring, it is actually the midpoint of the *traditional* season of spring, which stretches between Imbolc (1 February) and Beltane (1 May). The equinox is the time of conception, when the rising light overcomes darkness. This quality was acknowledged by the church as the festival of the Annunciation of the Blessed Virgin Mary (25 March, Lady Day). Alban Eilir is the time when the earth goddess Bride, married at Imbolc, conceives the sky god's child, which is due to be born at midwinter. It is also the time of the Asatru festival of Summer Finding, sacred to Thor, among other things the god of farm work. Freyr and Freya are also honored here. The traditional food for the Alban Eilir festival is a plum pudding, symbolic of the fruits of the previous season and known as the harvest strengthener. The associated sigil for the vernal equinox is a circle with two sprouting horns, signifying the seed putting forth its first springtime shoots.

May Day, or Beltane, commencing at sunset on 30 April, is the next festival. The divinity ruling Beltane is the solar fire deity, variously named Balor, Bel, Belenos, and Baldur, but it is also the time of all deities of growth and fecundity. The sacred color is white. The Asatru god Bragi and the goddess Iduna are associated with this feast. This time, including May Eve and Walpurgis Night, is a magical time, when the Beltane fires are kindled and revels held in celebration of the oncoming summertime. Then, it is customary to leap through the smoke and flames to purify oneself in preparation for the coming summer season and to promote fertility. The Beltane fire is traditionally composed of wood taken from nine different types of trees and is kindled on a specially prepared sacred grid. This is made by drawing a square on the ground and dividing it into nine smaller squares. Turf from the eight outer squares is dug out and removed, but the ninth is left at the center. The Beltane fire is lit upon the central square by turning an oaken spindle in an oak log socket—the ancient way of generating fire. Formerly, it was customary to extinguish all of the fires in the locality on May Eve. These were then relit from the village's Beltane fire. Burning at the center of the nine-square grid, the Beltane fire symbolized the central hearth of the community. These local sacred hearths represented the mystic divine fire at the center of all things, whose spark of life is carried by each of us. The traditional food for May Eve is the May cake, made from oatmeal and inscribed with the same grid pattern as the Beltane hearth.

May Day itself is associated with the maypole that is cut and brought in on the day before. Made from the wood of the birch, the tree of

 purification, the maypole is danced around in imitation of the twirling of the spindle used in the kindling of the Beltane fire. Rural merrymaking on May Day was absorbed into the urban landscape after the Industrial Revolution as the socialist Labor Day celebrated in many countries today. The flowers, flags, garlands, and maybushes (hawthorns) that bedecked country cottages and carts were transformed into the urban May Day banners of trade unions and political movements. Beltane's sigil is the Northern Tradition Tree of Life with six side branches, resembling a maypole and maybushes.

Litha, Alban Hefin, and Midsummer are all names for the summer solstice, on or about 21 June. The Litha festival period starts at Beltane, described above, and runs to Lammas (see below). The solstice day is the midpoint of summer, when the sun is above the horizon for the longest period, has its northernmost rising and setting, and its highest elevation at noon. It is the apex of the sun's splendor, the longest day and the shortest night.

The festival of Alban Hefin is sacred to the Great Mother goddess, sometimes personified as Cerridwen. In Asatru, it is sacred to the Norse

god Balder the Beautiful. Thor and his consort Sif are also remembered at the solstice. Midsummer was commemorated in medieval times as the feast of St. John the Baptist. In a continuation of Pagan tradition, bonfires were kindled on his day on the highest points in the district, to celebrate the highest point of the sun. If a fire is lit to celebrate Litha, it should be kindled on the windward side of any buildings, gardens, or fields that it is intended to bless, so that the purifying smoke can waft over them. At Litha, it is customary to burn flaming sunwheels, to swing burning brands in circles at the ends of chains, or to roll blazing tar barrels down slopes or through streets. Burning torches are carried in a sunwise direction around buildings, gardens, or fields to ensure good fortune. Midsummer is the time of fairs and festivals, and the great Midsummer Fair held on Midsummer Common at Cambridge, one of the largest in England, flourishes annually. From time immemorial festivals were also held at midsummer at Stonehenge, until they were suppressed by force in 1986. The traditional sigil for midsummer is an open curve that represents the open leaves of the plant, fully developed.

Lammas, Lughnassadh, or La Lunasa, 1 August, is sometimes celebrated as a two-day festival beginning on 31 July, a day sacred to Loki and Sigyn. August 1 is also sacred to Odin and Frigg. The traditional color of the autumn season that begins now is brown and the sigil is a semicircle bisected by a line. The grain harvest at Lughnassadh, which runs until Samhain, is the first of the three harvests of the natural year. (For the second and third see Mabon and Samhain below.) It is named after the Celtic god of wisdom and illumination, Lugh, equivalent in some aspects to the Anglo-Saxon god Woden and the Norse Odin. Lughnassadh represents the transformation of the goddess into the aspect of the pregnant Earth Mother. The Anglo-Saxon name of this festival is Hlafmesse ("loaf mass"), which celebrates the cutting of the first corn harvests and the baking of the loaf from the new year's crop. As the beginning of autumn, it heralds the gradual transformation of the child-bearing mother into the old woman who manifests fully at the next harvest festival, Samhain.

Mabon, Alban Elfed, or the autumnal equinox, on or about 23 September, is the point of transition between the light and the dark halves of the year and the beginning of solar decrease. As at Ostara, sunrise on

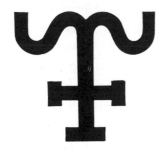 Mabon is due east and sunset due west. It is the time of the second harvest, that of fruits, marking the middle of the season of autumn. In ancient Greece, this was the time of the greater Eleusinian mysteries. It is sacred to the Greek goddesses Demeter and Persephone, and the Irish goddess Carman, patroness of poetry. In Asatru observance, the equinox is the festival of Winter Finding, sacred to the Norse fertility god, Frey. The traditional sigil for this equinox is of a stylized dying plant.

Samhain or Samhuinn, 1 November, marks the beginning of winter, at which time it was customary to slaughter livestock. Its eve marked the end of the old year in the Celtic calendar, and its dawn the beginning of the new year. Samhain is thus a time between the years and between the worlds, when the veil between the present and the past, the living and the dead, is thin. It is the Festival of the Dead, that time of year when we remember our ancestors and hail our descendents. In the Christian tradition, 1 November celebrates all of the departed saints, while 2 November remembers the souls of all the dead not elevated to sainthood. Materially, the nature of the festival, as with many other celebrations, is the same in the Pagan and the Christian traditions.

The festival of Samhain is celebrated widely on its eve. This is the Christianized festival of All Hallows' Eve, popularly known as Halloween, which is observed after dark on 31 October. The paper masks, rubber bats, plastic skeletons, and mock witches' hats of present-day Halloween parties are a modern expression of the Pagan festival of remembrance of death and the departed. In the natural year, Samhain is the third harvest when in former days animals were slaughtered and their meat smoked or salted down for winter. The tangible link with the dead at Samhain is present in the custom of making divinations on Halloween. Some Asatru groups remember the dark side of divinity at this festival in the forms of the dragons Fafnir and Hela, who were goddesses of the underworld.

In ancient Pagan Ireland, Samhain Day itself, La Samhna, was the middle day of a week's celebrations at which the high king would receive representatives of his nation bearing examples of their arts and crafts. This holy week of Samhain has given rise to a number of festivals around early

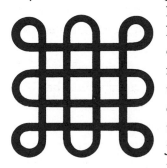 November. The celebration of Guy Fawkes Night, when an effigy of a seventeenth-century would-be regicide is burned, is also directly related to the older fire festival. The central focus of Guy Fawkes Night is the bonfire, continuing the practice of incinerating effigies that represent the ills and sadnesses of the year just passed. In Britain Remembrance Day, 11 November, commemorates the fallen of World War I and is also related to the earlier Celtic festival of the dead. It is held on the festival of Martinmas, otherwise known as Old November Day. The traditional sigil for the festival of Samhain is a knot of protection.

Yule, Alban Arthuan, or the winter solstice occurs on or about 21 December. The festival of Yuletide is composed of a number of separate, but related, celebrations. These begin with the Mother Night, starting at sunset on 20 December. This is one of the major festivals of Asatru, sacred to Odin, Ing, and Erda. The day of Yule is when the sun has reached its lowest ebb and is above the horizon for the shortest period in the year, making the shortest day flanked on either side by the longest nights. At this time, the sun rises and sets at its most southerly points, and it is at its lowest elevation at midday. The day of the winter solstice thus has the least sunlight, and that from the lowest elevation.

The name Yule, derived from the Anglo-Saxon *geola*, means the "yoke" of the year, the balance point across which travels the lowest ebb of sunlight. Even at its lowest ebb, however, it contains within itself the promise of lengthening days once more. Symbolically, then, Yule marks the rebirth of the sun's power. In the Roman tradition it was the festival of Sol Invictus, the Undefeated Sun. In several major religions, the birth of the chief god, identified with the sun, has been celebrated at this time. The Egyptian sky goddess Nut was said to give birth to the sun at the winter solstice, and the birthday of the sun-son in many religions, including Horus, Helios, Dionysos, Mithras, and Jesus, has been celebrated on 25 December, the old date of the winter solstice. The common feature of these midwinter divinities is that all are associated with concepts of rebirth and eternal life. The origin of Yule is clearly in the observance of the winter solstice, but it has been extended into a whole season of festivities. Tied to a calendar date, 25 December, the main festival of Yuletide has fallen out of synchronization with the actual solar phenomenon that it was originally intended to celebrate.

The long sequence of holy days around Yule is related to the old Roman celebration of Saturnalia, a time of intense merrymaking. The Yule festivities, which begin just before the winter solstice, include the blank day of the Celtic tree calendar (23 December), continue with Christmas Eve, Christmas Day, and Boxing Day (in Britain a day for giving

boxes—gifts—to servants), and incorporate New Year's Eve and New Year's Day. New Year's Eve (starting at sunset on 31 December) is known in Scotland by the Pagan name of Hogmanay, after the Celtic solar deity known variously as Hogmagog, Gogmagog, or Ogmios. The Yule festival ends at Twelfth Night, when the final trappings of Yuletide must be removed. In the circle of twenty-four runes, this time of year is ruled by the rune Jara, which has the meaning of the completion of the year, the enjoyment of the fruits of the harvest at the Yuletide feast. Of course, the major event of Yuletide is the feast itself, where all manner of food and drink is consumed. Yuletide is without doubt the major sacred meal of the year, a continuing expression of the Pagan holy feast tradition. The traditional sigil of Yuletide is an enclosure containing dots, symbolizing the seed in the ground, or people sheltering from the wintry weather.

The Stations of the Year

The eight festivals of the natural year are closely related to the stations of
the year, days that express the cycle of life and death inherent in the
agricultural round. Based on the harvest year, the stations of the year are
also a broad way of understanding the sequential nature of the processes
of life and death and the pathway to spiritual enlightenment. The first
station is not fixed; it is a mystery that cannot be defined—like the time of
a person's conception. But the first station is "located" somewhere between
Lammas and the autumnal equinox.

Stations of the Year (East Anglian Tradition)

STATION	FESTIVAL	EVENT	AGRICULTURAL CYCLE
1		Death/rebirth	Plant produces seed and dies
2	Autumnal Equinox	Calling/summoning	Fruit ripens/harvest
3	Samhain	Awakening	Letting go, seed is released from fruit
4	Yule	Enlightenment	Rebirth of the spark of life in the seed
5	Vernal Equinox	Reconciliation	Seed, apparently dead, comes back to life
6	Beltane	Mystic union	Plant grows in harmony with environment
7	Midsummer	Sanctification	Flower opens and is fertilized
8	Lammas	Completion	The circle turns

The Stations of the Day

These stations relate the times of day and their corresponding times of
the year to the various qualities of the eternal cycle of life. The stations
of the day comprise a more mystical or esoteric overview of the processes occurring within the day. It will be seen that symbolically, some
of the following stations tie in with the earlier table showing the tides
of the day.

Stations of the Day

STATION	TIME	EVENT
1	16:30	Death/rebirth; the parent plant brings forth the seed and prepares to die
2	18:00	Calling; the ripening of the fruit and its harvest
3	21:00	Awakening; the letting go; the seed falls from its mother to the earth
4	00:00	Enlightenment; the rebirth of the light in the darkness, the living seed, buried
5	06:00	Reconciliation; apparently dead, the seed comes to life again
6	09:00	Mystical union; the plant in its full flow of growth in harmony with the environment
7	12:00	Sanctification; the flower opens and is fertilized
8	15:00	Completion

Because they correspond with a time of day as well as a time of year, the stations of the daily cycle can be taken as a framework on which to base a cycle of corresponding meditational activities or sacred devotions.

The year is also divided into twelve periods ruled by signs of the zodiac. Each has both everyday and esoteric associations that are especially appropriate and powerful. A selection of these associations follows.

The Zodiac's Correspondences

ZODIAC SIGN	RULING PLANET	NORTHERN DEITY	WEEK DAY	PRECIOUS STONE	ANIMAL	COLOR	RUNIC LETTER
Capricorn	Saturn	Loki	Thur	Turquoise	Goat	Brown	Peorth (P)
Aquarius	Uranus	Urd	Sat	Amethyst	Eagle	Dark blue	Sigel (S)
Pisces	Neptune	Aegir	Thur	Bloodstone	Fish	White	Beorc (B)
Aries	Mars	Tyr	Tues	Diamond	Sheep	White	Ehwaz (E)
Taurus	Venus	Frigg	Fri	Sapphire	Bull	Yellow	Ing (Ng)
Gemini	Mercury	Odin	Wed	Emerald	Raven	Red	Dag (D)
Cancer	Moon	Mani	Mon	Agate	Crab	Green	Ur (U)
Leo	Sun	Sol	Sun	Ruby	Lion	Gold	As (A)
Virgo	Mercury	Odin	Wed	Sardonyx	Cat	Blue	Ken (K)
Libra	Venus	Frigg	Fri	Chrysolite	Serpent	Violet	Wyn (V)
Scorpio	Mars	Tyr	Tues	Opal	Scorpion	Red-brown	Nyd (N)
Sagittarius	Jupiter	Thor	Thur	Topaz	Aurochs	Orange	Jara (J)

Other Calendars

Three other fixed calendars are included in this book: the Celtic tree calendar, the runic half-month calendar, and the goddess calendar.

The Celtic Tree Calendar

The Celtic tree calendar is based on ogham, the ancient Irish and British tree alphabet. Each letter has a corresponding tree and color as well as a bird, herb, and so on. (For more details see my *Secret Lore of Runes and Other Ancient Alphabets*, Rider, 1991.) The periods of each month are calculated to the nearest day and are sufficient for most general purposes. For local sunset times—the exact end and beginning points between the months— ·

consult an almanac or ephemeris and adjust for real time. The new tree month begins on the eve of the day given in the calendar.

Celtic Tree Calendar

Luis (Rowan)	21 January-17 February
Nuin (Ash)	18 February-17 March
Fearn (Alder)	18 March-14 April
Saille (Willow)	15 April-12 May
Huath (Hawthorn)	13 May-9 June
Duir (Oak)	10 June-7 July
Tinne (Holly)	8 July-4 August
Coll (Hazel)	5 August-1 September
Muin (Vine)	2-29 September
Gort (Ivy)	30 September-27 October
Ngetal (Reed)	28 October-24 November
Ruis (Elder)	25 November-22 December
The Secret of the Unhewn Stone	23 December
Beth (Birch)	24 December-20 January

The Runic Half-Months

In this Pagan calendar and in most old records there is reference to runic half-months, times during which the particular corresponding qualities of the rune are said to be especially active. These run for the following periods:

Runic Half-Months

Eoh (yew tree)	28 December-12 January
Peorth (womb, dice cup)	13-27 January
Elhaz (elk)	28 January-11 February
Sigel (sun)	12-26 February
Tyr (cosmic pillar)	27 February-13 March
Beorc (birch tree)	14-29 March
Ehwaz (horse)	30 March-13 April

Runic Half-Months (continued)

Man (human being)	14-28 April
Lagu (flowing water)	29 April-13 May
Ing (expansive energy)	14-28 May
Odal (home, possession)	29 May-13 June
Dag (day)	14-28 June
Feoh (wealth)	29 June-3 July
Ur (primal strength)	14-28 July
Thorn (defense)	29 July-12 August
As (gods)	13-28 August
Rad (motion)	29 August-12 September
Ken (illumination)	13-27 September
Gyfu (gift)	28 September-12 October
Wyn (joy)	13-27 October
Hagal (constraint)	28 October-12 November
Nyd (necessity)	13-27 November
Is (stasis)	28 November-12 December
Jara (year)	13-27 December

The Goddess Calendar

The goddess calendar that appears in this book is the one popularized by Lux Madriana, the Fellowship of Isis, a Pagan group centered at Clonagal Castle in Enniscorthy, Ireland. Although it is somewhat recent, it is based on the Greco-Roman tradition. The goddess months are as follows:

The Goddess Calendar

Hestia	26 December–22 January
Bridhe	23 January–19 February
Moura	20 February–19 March
Columbina	20 March–17 April
Maia	18 April–15 May
Hera	16 May–12 June
Rosea	13 June–10 July
Kerea	11 July–8 August
Hesperis	9 August–5 September
Mala	6 September–2 October
Hathor	3–30 October
Cailleach/Samhain	31 October–27 November
Astraea	28 November–25 December

January

January is sacred to the Roman god Janus, the two-faced divinity of endings and beginnings. Janus is the male equivalent of one of the versions of the goddess Juno-Janus, who in her two-faced aspects of Antevorta and Postvorta looks simultaneously forward and backward, as does Janus. January marks the beginning of the new year yet contains elements of that which went before. Its quality is thus one of new possibilities but constrained by that which took place in the old year before it. In modern Asatru, this month is known as Snowmoon. In the American backwoods tradition the full moon of January is called the Wolf Moon. The backwoods names for the full moon derive from early New England settlers and trappers and Native American traditions.

The Celtic tree-calendar system uses some of the letters of the ogham alphabet, each of which has a corresponding tree. The first twenty days of January lie in the tree-calendar month of Beth, the birch tree, representing beginnings and purification. In the Celtic tradition, the sacred color of this month is white, and it is dedicated to the mother goddess. From 21 January, the ruling Celtic tree is the rowan, Luis. This has the sacred color of gray and is dedicated to Morrigan.

Other Pagan traditions have different divisions; in the fixed thirteen-month goddess calendar of Lux Madriana, January contains parts of the month of Hestia (until 22 January) and the beginning of the month of Bridhe.

Each month has a corresponding birthstone, whose virtues and powers are especially relevant to people born during that month. The January stone is the garnet. For each month there are orally handed down adages:

By her who in this month was born,
No gem save

Garnets should be worn.
They will ensure her constancy,
True friendship and fidelity.

A summerish January,
A winterish spring.
A January spring
Is worth nae thing.
If you see grass in January,
Lock your grain in your granary.

These lines speak of the false starts that sometimes happen in a warm January, where any young growth is almost certainly damaged by later frosts. If crops come up too early, shortages will follow. The weather of the first twelve days of the year is said to be indicative of that to be expected in the following twelve months. This traditional view formerly applied to the first twelve days of April but was later transferred to January. Moveable feasts in January include Plough Monday and St. Distaff's Day, the Monday and Tuesday following Twelfth Night (6 January), traditional days for returning to work after the Yule celebration. Another movable day is the Disting Moon, the full moon between Yule and Old Disting (25 January). The first day of the month is called the Kalends.

1 January

Kalends of January/New Year's Day/Fortuna/Jupiter/Juno/Egyptian Day

K
F

Ring out the old,
Ring in the new,
Ring out the false,
Ring in the true.

New Year's Day. Sacred to the Greek divine pair Zeus and Hera, the Roman Jupiter and Juno. Also day of offering to the goddess

Fortuna (left) in order that the new year should be beneficial to all. Pictured below (page 28) is a medieval representation of New Year's "guising."

2 January

Advent of Isis/Nativity of Our Lady Inanna/Egyptian Day

 Nativity of Our Lady Inanna, the Sumerian goddess who is princess of the earth and queen of heaven. As goddesses of love, Isis and Inanna are related to Aphrodite, Astarte, Ishtar, and Cybele.

As the weather is on the second of January, so it will be in September.

3 January

St. Genevieve/Customary Kalends of January

Customary Kalends of January (in the East Anglian tradition) dedicated to St. Genevieve, patroness or *genius loci* of the city of Paris.

> *If January Kalends be summerly gay,*
> *'Twill be wintry weather till the*
>   *Kalends of May.*

4 January

Egyptian Day

5 January
Nones of January

N

6 January
Twelfth Night/Epiphany of Kore-Persephone/Christian Epiphany

Twelfth Night, when the debris of the Yule feast must be cleared away. In the Julian (Old Style) calendar it is Old Christmas Day. The nocturnal rite in honor of Kore was held overnight 5–6 January in the Koreion at Alexandria. It was a mystic drama preparing the way for Kore/Persephone's rise into the world.

7 January
Sekhmet, Ancient Egyptian New Year's Day

8 January
Justitia/ ☽ Disting Moon

A day sacred to Justitia, Roman goddess of justice.

9 January

10 January

Geraint

A day sacred to the ninth-century Welsh bard, Geraint, the Blue Bard of Wales.

11 January

Carmentalia/Juturna/ ☽ *Plough Monday*

First festival of the Roman Carmentalia, celebrating the nymphs of prophecy known as the Camenae, who are identified with the nine Muses. The chief of these was Carmentis, the goddess of prophecy, who also protected women in childbirth. Also on this day Juturna, divinity of fountains and

prophetic waters and patroness of all who work with water, was worshiped in ancient Rome. Also, Plough Monday, traditional day for returning to work in the fields. Farm workers received plough money; children, handsel in the form of money or sweets from neighbors.

12 January

Compitalia/The Lares/ ☽ *St. Distaff's Day*

Roman festival of Compitalia celebrates the household gods, the Lares. On St. Distaff's Day, named after a sanctified tool rather than an individual, women would resume their spinning after Yule. The day is sacred to the chief goddess of Old England, Frigg (right), whose followers were called the Freefolk. Although she is associated with the distaff, not all areas of life under her guidance are about work:

Partly work and partly play,
Ye must on Saint Distaff's Day.

13 January

Ides of January/Tiugunde Day/Midvintersblót/St. Hilary/New Year's Day in the Julian calendar/Runic half-month of Peorth commences

I In some places, New Year's observances such as was-sailing (paying homage to apple trees) are still performed on this day. Day of the Norse ceremony of Midvintersblót, Midwinter's Offering, called Tiugunde Day in Old England and sacred to Tiu, the ancient Teutonic chief god, ruler of the year. This day falls twenty days after Yule.

14 January

15 January

Carmentalia (second festival)/Egyptian Day

16 January

Concordia

The goddess Concordia, principle of harmonious relations with all, is honored.

17 January

Felicitas/Egyptian Day

Sacred to Felicitas, a minor Roman goddess of good luck.

18 January

19 January

20 January

St. Agnes' Eve/Celtic tree month of Beth ends

Traditionally, St. Agnes' Day is a time for divination by fire.

21 January

St. Agnes/Celtic tree month of Luis commences

22 January

St. Vincent/Goddess month of Hestia ends

St. Vincent is a Christianization of the sun god Apollo, whose emblem is

pictured at left. Of the weather marker known as St. Vincent's Day:

> Remember on St. Vincent's Day
> If that the sun his beams display,
> Be sure to mark his transient beam
> Which through the window sheds a gleam;
> For 'tis a token bright and clear,
> Of prosperous weather all the year.

23 January

Goddess month of Bridhe commences

At right is St. Bridget's cross, a traditional symbol of protection.

24 January

Cornish Tinners' and Seafarers' Day/St. Paul's Eve

Cornish Tinner's and Seafarer's Day is an old "labor day," celebrating the new season of sailing and mining in Cornwall. In the old wooden calendars known as clog almanacks (right), rimstocks, or prime-staves, each eve or aften was marked by the letter A.

25 January

Old Disting/Burns' Night/St. Paul's Day

Important in old runic calendars, Disting is the feast of the Disir, the Norse guardian goddesses. On this day a major festival of the gods was held at the temple in Uppsala, Sweden (right). Burns' Night celebrates Robert Burns, the Scots poet. Burns' Night revels are a modern continuation of Disting. The day is also a weather marker:

If St. Paul's Day be fair and clear,
It do betide a happy year.
But if it chance to snow or rain,
Then will be dear all kinds of grain.
If clouds or mists do dark the sky,
Great store of birds and beasts will die.
And if the winds do fly aloft,
Then wars shall vex the kingdom oft.

If it should thunder on St. Paul's Day, great winds are predicted.

26 January

27 January

28 January

Runic half-month of Elhaz commences

This half-month is a period of optimistic power, protection, and sanctuary.

29 January

Egyptian Day

ⵏ

30 January

Festival of Peace

Festival of peace, dedicated to the Roman goddess Pax.

31 January

February Eve/Norns/Disir and Valkyries

February Eve, start of the festival of Imbolc or Brigantia. Also a day sacred to the Valkyries, pictured at right, and the Norns, below, shown seated beneath Yggdrasil, the world tree.

february

The name of this month comes from the Roman goddess Februa, mother of Mars. Known also as Juno Februa and St. Febronia (from Febris, the fever of love), she is the patroness of the passion of love. In the Northern Tradition, she is the Norse goddess Sjofn. Her orgiastic rites are celebrated on 14 February—still observed as St. Valentine's Day—when, in Roman times, young men would draw billets naming their female partners. The Irish name for February is Feabhra, and the Anglo-Saxon name for this month was Solmonath, "sun

month," noting the gradual return of the light after the darkness of midwinter. In the ancient Frankish and the modern Asatru calendars, February is Horning, from Horn, the turn of the year. In the American backwoods tradition, the full moon in February is called the Snow Moon. February is the shortest month, according to legend having had a day looted by the month of August. Originally, it appears that the months were arranged alternately with thirty-two and thirty days. But at some point, this was altered, and February was truncated, becoming two days shorter than the others, except in the bissextile or leap year.

The Celtic tree-calendar month of Luis, the rowan, runs until 17 February. It is superseded on the 18th by Nuin, the ash tree. The ash is the linking axis between the worlds and its color is clear, like glass. It is sacred to Gwydion, who, as god of wisdom, parallels the Teutonic divinity Woden, otherwise called Odin. This is a time of clear vision into other worlds, expressed by festivals of purification. On 1 February is the celebration of the cross-quarter day or fire festival, Imbolc (Oimelc) or Brigantia, a purificatory festival. It is followed on the 2nd by its Christian counterpart, Candlemas, the Purification of the Blessed Virgin Mary. Later in the month, 19 February and 21 February are, respectively, the Roman Parentalia and Feralia, likewise festivals of purification. The goddess-calendar month of Bridhe fills most of February, ending on the 19th. February 20 sees the beginning of the month of Moura. The birthstone of February is the amethyst:

If the February-born shall find
Sincerity and peace of mind,
Freedom from passion and from care,
If she the Amethyst will wear.

Country weather lore calls this month February fill-dyke, indicating a good deal of snow or rain is to be expected:

February, fill the dyke,
Either with the black or white.
If it's white, the better to like.

It is thought that a snowy month means that the spring will be fine.

When February give much snow,
A fine summer dost foreshow.

A mild and sunny February is thought to be a bad omen, presaging a wet and stormy summer:

Of all the months in the year
Curse a fair Februeer.

1 February

Cross-quarter day: Imbolc, Oimelc, Brigantia/Kalends of February/St. Bridget/ Candemas Eve

K Imbolc is the fire festival between Yule and the vernal equinox. The day of Imbolc is also that of her saintly aspect, St. Bridhe or Brigid of Ireland. A St. Bridget's knot is to the left.

2 February

Juno Februa/Candlemas/Wives' Feast Day/Groundhog Day

Festival of Juno Februa, the presiding goddess of the month, and Candlemas, the purification of the Virgin. The weather on this day is said to mark the progress of winter:

> *If Candlemas Day be fair and bright,*
> *Winter will have another flight;*
> *If on Candlemas Day be shower and rain,*
> *Winter is gone, and will not come again.*

Also,

> *If the sun shines bright on Candlemas Day,*
> *The half of the winter's not yet away.*

These sayings agree with those about Groundhog Day that link the length of winter to whether or not the groundhog sees his shadow on this day. An old northern English name of Candlemas is the Wives' Feast Day.

3 February

St. Blasius

St. Blasius or Blaise was one of the Fourteen Holy Helpers and is invoked in the case of sick cattle. The blessing of St. Blaise  for sufferers from throat disease is held to be most efficacious if performed on his patronal day. Above is a knot of protection.

4 February

King Frost Day

On this day in 1814, a fair was held in London in honor of King Frost on the river Thames, which was completely frozen over. The celebration of King Frost Day died out during World War I.

5 February

Nones of February/Tyche/Fortuna/Wyrd/St. Agatha

N St. Agatha is an aspect of the goddess known to the Greeks as Tyche, to the Romans as Fortuna (right), and to the Anglo-Saxons as Wyrd. This day is especially potent for fortune telling and all forms of divination.

6 February

St. Dorothea

St. Dorothea's Day, a day said to bring snow.

7 February

8 February

Egyptian Day

9 February

Apollo/St. Apollonia

Feast day of Apollo (right), the deity of the sun. It celebrates the increasing light of the new year after the darkness of midwinter.

10 February

Egyptian Day

11 February

Our Lady/Egyptian Day

The date in 1858 of the famous apparition of Our Lady at Lourdes. This was the last manifestation at a grotto which, for many centuries, had been known as a shrine of the goddess.

12 February

Artemis/Diana/Runic half-month of Sigel commences

Holy day of the divine huntress, the goddess Artemis or Diana. The runic half-month of Sigel commences here. It represents the power of the force of good throughout the world and is the harbinger of victory and ascendancy over darkness.

13 February

Ides of February/Parentalia/St. Matthias/Old Leap Year's Day

The Parentalia was the chief Roman festival of the dead which lasted until the Feralia on 21 February. St. Matthias took the place of Judas as the twelfth apostle. This is his traditional East Anglian feast day.

14 February

Juno Februa/Vali/St. Valentine

St. Valentine's Day is a festival of love that amal-
gamates the Pagan traditions of Rome and north-
ern Europe. It is also dedi-
cated to the Norse deity
Vali, the archer god,
son of Odin, and to
Juno Februa (right),

goddess of maternal and married love. The
festival begins after sunset on 13 February.
Girls should decorate their pillows with five bay
leaves, to dream of their lover and husband-to-
be. In England on this day an arch of brambles is carried to banish unwelcome spirits. In Scandinavia there is a tradition of running labyrinths
on this day.

15 February

Faunus/Lupercalia/Sigfrid/St. Oswy

Lupercalia is an ancient festival of Roman
Paganism. Ovid ascribes this festival to the
rustic god Faunus, protector of agriculture
and flocks, giver of oracles, and an aspect of
the great god
Pan. This is a
day when ani-
mals help hu-
mans. It also
celebrates the
she-wolf who
suckled the
infants Romulus and Remus. In the Odinist
calendar this day is sacred to the hero
Sigfrid.

16 February

17 February

Fornacalia/Celtic tree month of Luis ends/Egyptian Day

 Roman festival of Fornacalia, festival of bread, ovens, and the oven goddess. It is also a festival whose observance helps plants in their coming growing season. On this day, plants should be tended with extra loving care.

18 February

Festival of Women/Celtic tree month of Nuin commences/Tacita/Egyptian Day

 This day is a Persian Pagan festival honoring women. Also the day of Roman rites in honor of Tacita, the silent goddess, binding hostile speech and unfriendly mouths.

19 February

Goddess month of Bridhe ends

20 February

Goddess month of Moura commences

21 February

Feralia

During the Roman Feralia, the spirits of the dead were

believed to be abroad in the world, hovering above their graves. Provisions were left at graves for them. This was the last day of the Roman year for placating ghosts; on 22 February the living were appeased.

22 February

Concordia/Charistia

Roman festival of the goddess Concordia, the feast of favor or goodwill, known as the Charistia. It is the time for the living to reconcile their differences, the counterpart of Feralia on the previous day. It is also time for a meal with family and friends, at which all disputes are settled.

23 February

Terminalia

Roman festival of Terminalia, when Terminus, god of boundaries, is acknowledged. At right is a runic boundary stone from Sweden.

24 February

25 February

26 February

Egyptian Day

27 February

Runic half-month of Tyr commences/Egyptian Day

 This is a time of positive regulation, when one must make sacrifices and work hard in order to progress.

28 February

29 February

Leap Year's Day (1996, 2000)/Egyptian Day

 In the old tradition this is a day when women can propose marriage to men.

march

The month of March is sacred to the Roman god
Mars, whose equivalents are the Greek Ares and the
old sky god of central and northern Europe, Tiu or
Tiwaz. In northern and western Europe, this deity is
known as the Celtic god Teutates and as the Norse
god Tyr. His original name was Mavors. After Jupiter, Mars was the chief Roman god, often known as
Marspater, Father Mars. He was worshiped at Rome
as god of war, but he was also the protector of "the
most honorable pursuit," agriculture. Like many goddesses, Mars also appears under three aspects. As the
martial god, he was Gradivus; as the rustic god,
Silvanus; and as patron of the Roman state, Quirinus. He and his consort,
Neria, whose name means "strong," are commemorated on 25 March. The
wolf and the woodpecker are sacred to Mars. In Ireland, the month of
March is Mi an Mharta, also honoring the god Mars. The Anglo-Saxon
name of this month was Hrethmonath, "Hertha's month," commemorating the Earth Mother goddess Hertha or Nerthus. Containing the vernal
equinox, also called Alban Elir and Ostara, March is a month of renewal.
This aspect of growth is present in the Frankish name for March,
Lentzinmanoth, literally, "renewal month." Modern Asatru calls March
Lenting. The full moon of this month is called the Worm or Sap Moon in
the American backwoods tradition.

     The first part of March is occupied by the Celtic tree month of Nuin,
or ash. On 18 March, this gives way to Fearn, the alder month. This is a tree
of protection against conflict. Its sacred color is crimson. In the goddess
calendar, the month of Moura ends on 19 March. The next month,
Columbina, begins on the 20th. March's birthstone is the bloodstone:

Who on this world of ours their eyes
In March first o'en shall be wise,

In days of peril, firm and brave,
And wear a Bloodstone to their grave.

The weather in March is said to begin and end in opposite ways. If the month comes in like a lion, it will go out like a lamb, and vice versa. Another adage is enshrined in the couplet:

So many mists in March you see
So many frosts in May will be.

Naturally, as the first notably springlike month, March is seen as a key month for later fertility, for, "A wet March makes a sad harvest," and "A peck of March dust and a shower in May. Make the corn green and the meadows gay," and "A peck of March dust is worth a king's ransom." Also "March winds and April showers bring forth May flowers." But "March flowers make no summer bowers." The Jewish holiday of Purim is a movable feast that often occurs in March.

1 March

Kalends of March/Matronalia/St. David/Roman New Year

K Roman women's festival of Matronalia, sacred to the goddess Juno Lucina. Prayers were offered for prosperity in marriage, and women received presents from men. The first of March is also a holy day in Wales, celebrating the patron saint, David, whose emblematic plants, the leek and daffodil, represent the vigorous growth of springtime and recall the royal colors, green and white, of ancient Britain.

2 March

Ceadda/St. Chad/Holy Wells Day

A day sacred to Ceadda, deity of healing springs and holy wells. His symbol is the Crann Bethadh, the tree of life. As a meditation, St. Chad was known to spend all night immersed up to his neck in a holy well, a Northern

Tradition technique. On this day one should honor a holy well by cleaning it and making an offering of flowers. Some loving care on Ceadda's day might reinvigorate many an abandoned sacred spring.

3 March

Aegir/St. Winnal

St. Winnal is a Christian version of Aegir, a Teutonic god of the sea. As controller of the sea's tides and weather, St. Winnal's holy day is associated with storms. When a Winnal storm occurs, this is March "coming in like a lion." It should presage a fine end to the month.

> *First comes David,*
> *Next comes Chad,*
> *Then comes Winnal,*
> *Roaring mad.*

Above is a medieval graffito of a hobbyhorse used in Morris dancing, which traditionally starts this time of year.

4 March

Egyptian Day

5 March

Navigium Isis

This ancient Egyptian festival recognized the goddess's invention of the sail and her patronage of sailing. It is observed as the beginning of the new sailing season.

6 March

Mars/St. Martian

On this day, the Roman household gods were honored. At right is Mars in a more peaceful aspect.

7 March

Junonalia/The Nones of March/ ☽ Purim

N This festival was observed by the Romans in honor of the goddess Juno. A procession of twenty-seven girls, dressed in long robes, accompanied the image of the goddess, carved from the wood of the cypress tree, which is sacred to her. It is also the Jewish spring festival of Purim.

8 March

9 March

10 March

11 March

Herakles/St. Hercules

Day of the semidivine hero Herakles

or Hercules. It is a day of strength and superhuman feats of courage.

12 March

Martyrdom of Hypatia

Commemorates the martyrdom of Hypatia, known as the Divine Pagan. Born in the year 370 C.E., she was dean of the Neoplatonic school at Alexandria. A famed philosopher and mathematician, she was murdered by a Christian death squad. At left is the owl of wisdom.

13 March

14 March

Veturius Mamurius/Runic half-month of Beorc commences/Egyptian Day

The festival of Veturius Mamurius celebrates the art of armor making. The half-month of Beorc is ruled by the goddess of the birch tree, a time of symbolic purification for rebirth and new beginnings.

15 March

Rhea/Anna Perenna/Ides of March

The Ides of March. This date is famous as that on which Julius Caesar was assassinated in 44 B.C.E. It is also a holy day of Rhea (right), Greek goddess of the earth, mother of Zeus, and an aspect of the Great Mother. Traditionally, river sprites or nymphs are acknowledged on the Ides of March.

16 March

Dionysus/Bacchus/Egyptian Day

Beginning of the two-day festival of the Greek god Dionysus, equivalent to the Roman Bacchus, youthful deity of wine. The festival promotes a fruitful grape harvest.

17 March

Dionysus/Bacchus/St. Patrick/Celtic tree month of Nuin ends/Egyptian Day

Trefuilnid Treochair, the national day of Ireland. The feast for "the triple bearer of the triple key," the trident-bearing Celtic divinity assimilated to St. Patrick, whose sacred plant is the shamrock.

18 March

St. Edward the Martyr/Celtic tree month of Fearn commences

 The Anglo-Saxon monarch Edward, king and martyr, was assassinated on the orders of his stepmother in the year 979 C.E., perhaps as part of a continuing tradition of the sacrificial king who must die for his people.

19 March

Athena/Minerva/Eyvind Kinnrifi/Goddess month of Moura ends

 The day before the equinox is one of the festivals of the Greek goddess Athena. In Roman times, this was the festival of the birth of the goddess Minerva (left), called Quinquatrus. Eyvind Kinnrifi was one  of Odin's martyrs; their symbol is the Valknut or knot of the slain, above.

20 March

☉ *Vernal Equinox: Alban Eilir, Ostara, Fifth Station of the Year/Iduna/ Goddess month of Columbina commences/Egyptian Day*

Today is also sacred to the Norse goddess Iduna, bearer of the magic apples of life who personifies the light half of the year. She appears on this day as a sparrow, bringing joy to humans.

21 March

Tea and Tephi

In Irish tradition, the holy city of Tara was founded on this day by the Milesian princesses Tea and Tephi.

22 March

23 March

Summer Finding

This Norse festival acknowledges the light of the sun becoming more powerful than darkness. Pictured at right are Thor, Odin, Heimdall, Sigyn, and Loki.

24 March

Britannia/Heimdall/Archangel Gabriel

Day of the guardian goddess of Albion (Great Britain), Prytania or Britannia, whose image appears on British coins. Also the day of the guardian of heaven, Heimdall, or the Archangel Gabriel (left). A day of orderliness. Above is the rune of protection.

25 March

Mars and Neria/Lady Day/Return of the Goddess

The festival of Lady Day (the Annunciation) celebrates the conception date of the divinity that enters the world on 25 December. Goddess worshipers call this day the Return of the Goddess. The 25 March was also once considered to be the date of the creation of the world. Pictured above is a drawing of one of the earliest representations of the goddess Freya from Schleswig Cathedral in Germany. The sigil at left is a traditional one for spring.

26 March

27 March

28 March

St. Mark's Eve/Sacrifice at the Tombs/Pallas

The treatise *De Pascha Comutus*, written in 243 C.E., states that the sun and moon were created on 28 March. Before the adoption of 25 December as the "correct" date (in 336 C.E. at Rome), this date was given as the date of the nativity of Jesus. Today is also the old Roman festival of Sacrifice at the Tombs, acknowledging the ancestors, as well as St. Mark's Eve. St. Mark is pictured at right.

29 March

St. Mark

The traditional feast day of St. Mark in East Anglia.

30 March

Janus and Concordia/Runic half-month of Ehwaz commences

Festival of Janus and Concordia. The runic half-month of Ehwaz, the horse, is a time of partnership between humans and nature, as between rider and horse. Good time for a pilgrimage.

31 March

Luna

Roman festival of Luna, goddess of the full moon whose temple on the Aventine hill was the focus of worship on this day.

april

The month of April is named after the Greek goddess Aphrodite (the Roman Venus). According to Ovid, it is "the fourth month, in which thou art honored above all others, and thou knowest, O Venus, that both the poet and the month are thine."

April is the season of opening. It is the month when the earth opens to receive seed, the time when the growing plants open up, the young leaves unfold, and the blossoms open. The Anglo-Saxon name for this month is Eastermonath, the month of the goddess Eostre, whose name is the origin of the word Easter. She can be seen as an aspect of Aphrodite. The Irish name for April is Aibrean; to the Franks, it was Ostarmanoth. Modern followers of Asatru call it Ostara. The backwoods' full moon that falls in April is called the Pink Moon.

April 1 is one of the few days that has widespread secular observance (the others being Halloween, Christmas, and New Year's). The custom of playing tricks and practical jokes on people on All Fools' Day, making them into April fools, is in the tradition of the trickster. In every stable society, in order that things should not become too rigid, there are periods when misrule is permitted for a short, well-defined time. In the Northern Tradition, the trickster god Loki is patron of 1 April. Although he is a being who causes much unwelcome trouble, he can perform tasks that no one else can do. In medieval times this function was performed by the royal jester. Sometimes, only the jester could provide the alternative viewpoint, telling the monarch that something was wrong with his or her rulership. He could speak truthfully, in jest, at times when no one else dared speak for fear of punishment. In the Tarot, the card called the Fool, carrying the number zero, fulfills this necessary role.

As the joker among customary festivals, All Fools' Day does not commence on the eve but at morning and only operates until midday. Apart from All Fools' Day, the beginning of April has few traditional festivals. The Celtic tree-calendar month of Fearn runs until 14 April. This is the Celtic tree letter of the alder, which signifies protection in times of conflict, stability in times of change. In the Norse calendar, Sommarsblót on 14 April marks the beginning of the summer half of the year, paralleled by Winter's Day (Vinternatsblót) on 14 October. Fearn is followed on 15 April by Saille, the willow month. This has the sacred color quality of "bright," and is connected with tidal energies, ruled by the moon. In the Goddess calendar, the month of Columbina runs until 17 April, the month dedicated to Maia following on 18 April. Passover and Easter are movable holy days that usually fall in April.

A birthstone adage for April concerns the diamond:

> *She who from April dates her years*
> *Diamonds should wear lest bitter tears*
> *For vain repentance flow; this stone*
> *As emblem of innocence is known.*

Traditional country weather lore knows the April weather to be changeable: "April weather, rain and sunshine both together." Cold weather in April is supposed to be good for a bumper harvest:

> *A cold April*
> *The barn will fill.*

This is reinforced by the sayings, "Rain in April will bring a good May," and "A wet April makes a dry June," but:

> *If the first three days in April be foggy,*
> *Rain in June will make the lanes boggy.*

1 April

Kalends of April/All Fools' Day/Fortuna Virilis/Loki

K Today it is socially permissible to play tricks and practical jokes until noon. April 1 is the classic Festival of Fools, ruled over by the Norse trickster god Loki. It is also the Roman women's festival of Fortuna Virilis, seeking good relations with men and ruled over by Venus.

2 April

3 April

4 April

Megalesia or Magna Mater

The first festival day of Megalesia/Magna Mater, or Cybele (right), the Great Mother, of whom all the goddesses may be seen as aspects. This seven-day festival celebrates the arrival of the image of Cybele in Rome from Asia Minor.

5 April

Megalesia/Fortuna/Nones of April

N Festival for good luck, celebrating the goddess Fortuna (right), the Lady Luck to whom all gamblers pray.

6 April

Megalesia/ ☽ Passover

Passover is the Jewish celebration of liberation from bondage in Egypt.

7 April

Megalesia/Egyptian Day

8 April

Megalesia/Egyptian Day

9 April

Megalesia

10 April

Megalesia/Egyptian Day

The final day of Megalesia was celebrated with sacred horse racing. Today, this once sacred sport is completely secularized, though it still carries sacred overtones in its title "the sport of kings." At right is a Gnostic representation of Fate.

11 April

☽ *Easter*

Easter is named for the goddess of spring, Eostre or Ostara.

12 April

Cerealia

Cerealia was the eight-day Roman festival of Ceres, goddess of the earth and its fruits, who was prayed to for peace, good government, and plenty.

13 April

Cerealia/Libertas/Ides of April

I The springtime festival of Libertas, the Roman goddess of Liberty.

14 April

Cerealia/Runic half-month of Man commences/ Sommarsblót/St. Tiburtius/Celtic tree month of Fearn ends

The Norse festival of Sommarsblót is celebrated to welcome the summer. The runic half-month of Man is a time when the archetypal reality of the human condition should be meditated upon.

15 April

Cerealia/Tellus/Celtic tree month of Saille commences

The old Roman festival of the goddess Tellus, often called Tellus Mater, Mother Earth, is traditionally devoted to prayer for the continued health of our environment. Tellus is the matron goddess of all environmentalists.

16 April

Cerealia/St. Padarn/Egyptian Day

Known by its Celtic dedication as St. Padarn's Day. On this day it was customary to begin weeding the growing crops.

17 April

Cerealia/Goddess month of Columbina ends/Egyptian Day

At right is an altar dedicated to Ceres.

18 April

Cerealia/Goddess month of Maia commences/Egyptian Day

19 April

Cerealia

20 April

Egyptian Day

F

21 April

Parilia/Earth Day/Egyptian Day

F The festival of the Roman pastoral deity, Pales, known as the Parilia, included decorating sheepfolds with green branches; kindling fires, through whose smoke the animals were driven; and offering milk and cakes to the divinity. In more recent times, it has become Earth Day, when people remember their responsibility toward the environment.

22 April

23 April

Jupiter and Venus/Sigurd/St. George

In Roman Paganism, today is the festival of

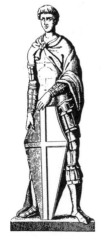

Jupiter and Venus. In England, it is dedicated to St. George, the country's patron saint. St. George's Day is the remnant of an ancient festival of fertility, the traditional day for parades of dragons, hobbyhorses, and giant effigies. St. George is a version of the Greek chimera-slayer, Bellerophon, and the northern European hero, Sigurd the Dragonslayer, the Siegfried of Wagner's opera. In English Asatru, it is the day of Sigurd, festival of the homeland. Above is a thirteenth- or fourteenth-century graffito of a morris dancer from Sutton in Bedfordshire and, at left, an image of St. George.

24 April

St. Mark's Eve

The eve of St. Mark's Day is one of the traditional nights for divining the future. Any young woman wishing to see her future lover should fast from sunset and then during the night make and bake a cake containing an eggshellful of salt, wheat meal, and barley meal. Then she should open the door of her dwelling place. Her future lover should come in and turn the cake. Above is a Gnostic image of Luna Regia, the moon goddess.

25 April

Robigalia/St. Mark/Cuckoo Day

St. Mark's Day is the old Roman festival of the Robigalia, the observance of which was magically intended to avert the spirit of mildew, which threatens crops around this time. For many years, the Litania Major of the Catholic church for St. Mark's Day at Rome followed the earlier festival. Its purpose, like the Robigalia, was to gain the blessing of heaven for the growing crops. In traditional English lore, this is Cuckoo Day. The cuckoo, "St. Mark's gowk," heralds the arrival of migratory birds from the south, indicating the return of summer.

26 April

27 April

28 April

Floralia

The three-day Roman festival of Floralia commemorates the goddess Flora, deity of flowers and the pleasures of youth. Her feast day was noted for its license, and medallions showing various positions of sexual enjoyment were distributed to the revelers. Beans and other seeds were thrown into the crowds, denoting fertility and fecundity.

29 April

Floralia/Runic half-month of Lagu commences

Representing the flowing and mutable—yet irresistably powerful and necessary—forces of water, Lagu symbolizes the life-force inherent in all matter and the organic growth and waxing power of this time of year.

30 April

Floralia/Salus/Walpurgis Night/May Eve/St. Sophia

May Eve is the festival of the dead in Portugal and Spain. In Germany it is Walpurgis Night, dedicated to the Saxon goddess, Walpurga. On Walpurgis Night, 1990, the Brocken, the German witches' holy mountain, was reclaimed by women's groups.

may

The merry month of May is named after the goddess who is chief of the Greek Seven Sisters (the Pleiades) and the mother of Hermes. In legend, it is said that Hermes himself bestowed his mother's name upon the month, Maia Majestas, goddess of spring. The Irish Celtic Queen Medb (Maeve) was an incarnation of this goddess. Later, she became the fairy Queen Mab of Shakespeare. Her sacred plant, the hawthorn, or may tree, blossoms during this month, which is one of vigorous growth. The Anglo-Saxon name of May was Thrimilcmonath, "thrice-milk month," be-cause cows give milk three times daily during the month of May. Another old English name for May is Sproutkale, conjuring up visions of luxuriant plant growth. The runes ruling this month are Lagu (L), which signifies vigorous, energetic growth, and Ing (Ng), representing fertility and procre-ation. The old Frankish name of the merry month, Winnemanoth, "joy month," describes our pleasure at the oncoming summer, as does the modern Asatru Merrymoon. The backwoods' full moon is the Flower Moon. May is the customary time for revels, the Maying ceremonies and traditional love games of May Day. As the first day of summer, May Day is one of the most important days of the year. It has many alternative names. One ancient Irish name was Cedsoman, which today has become Ceadamh, meaning literally "the first of summer." In Irish, May Day is La Bealtaine. The name Beltaine contains the element *taine*, which means "fire." The first element is that of the solar deity who is called variously Beli, Belinus, and Balder. One traditional name for the customary bonfires on May Eve is Balder's balefirs.

Beltane is station six of the year, mystical union. The maypole tradi-tion flourishes today in German-speaking countries, but because it was attacked ruthlessly by the authorities in Britain during the sixteenth and seventeenth centuries, it survives there in a much truncated form. Traditionally May is a month of the appearance on Earth of the mother goddess, whether as the Lady of Wiccas, Mother Mary, or the various corresponding goddesses of indigenous religious traditions. However she is perceived to manifest herself, she is Our Lady, representative of the archetypal mother. As the consort of Robin Hood, she is the Maid Marian of traditional Maytime revels.

The emerald is the birthstone of the month of May. The Celtic willow month of Saille ends on 12 May, followed by the hawthorn month, Huath. This brings protection of the inner and outer realms and is sacred to the hammer gods of thunder, Taranis, Thunor, and Thor. Its sacred color is purple. The goddess calendar month of Maia fills the first half of May, ending on the 15th. It is followed by Hera, which begins on 16 May. Movable holidays in May include Mjollnir, the festival of Thor's Hammer (celebrated on a Thursday and coinciding with Ascension Day in the Church calendar), and the commemoration of Buddha's enlightenment, which occurs on the day of the full moon in May.

Rain in May assists the full growth of the crops. This is recorded in the country adages "Water in May, bread all the year" and

Mist in May, heat in June,
Make the harvest come right soon.

1 May

Cross-quarter day: Beltane, May Day, Sixth Station of the
Year/Kalends of May

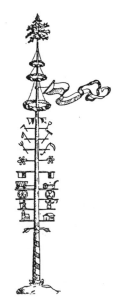

K This is one of the major Pagan festivals of the year. It signifies mystical union, the time when the plant is in full growth and in harmony with the environment.

2 May

Floralia/Elena/St. Helen

A day sacred to the goddess Elena. As Helen, she is the goddess of the holy road, more particularly, the four royal roads of Britain. In Wales the causeways and roads called Sarn Helen are her holy, old straight tracks. She is the Elaine of Arthurian romance.

3 May

Floralia/Bona Dea Eve/Egyptian Day

The eve of 4 May is the time sacred to Bona Dea, the Good Goddess in the Roman tradition important in women's mysteries, to whom offerings were made in secret.

4 May

Bona Dea/Veneration of the Thorn

The hawthorn tree, sacred to the Good Goddess, is honored on this day. The hawthorn is often called the white-thorn and, when it is flowering, the may tree. At the festival of the Veneration of the Thorn, holy bushes and trees—those marking sacred places and holy wells—are today acknowledged by having new scraps of cloth tied to them.

5 May

6 May

Eyvind Kelve/ ☽ Enlightenment of the Buddha/ Egyptian Day

The Norwegian Pagan martyr, Eyvind Kelve, was killed on the orders of King Olaf Trygvason for refusing to give up his faith in the Pagan gods. At left is the Irminsul, a Norse

symbol of the cosmos. The enlightenment of the Buddha (pictured above) is celebrated in many Buddhist traditions on the day of the full moon in May.

7 May

Nones of May/Helston Furry Dance/Egyptian Day

The famous Furry or Floral Dance is traditionally performed at Helston in Cornwall. In former times, dancing through towns and villages was commonplace.

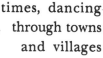

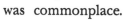

8 May

9 May

Lemuria

The Roman lemures are the wandering spirits of dead family members who revisit their former homes on this day. The shades are acknowledged on the three days of the Lemuria. The other two days when the spirits are abroad are 11 May and 13 May.

10 May

11 May

Lemuria/St. Mamertius

The days of the Eisheilige (ice saints), May 11-15, are noted in southern Germany as the time when the presence of these "Strong Lords" brings unseasonably cold and/or wet weather. These are the saints Mamertius, Pancratius (Pancras), Servatius, Bonifatius, and Cold Sophie. The names of these saints are Christianized versions of the Swabian presiding spirits of the days.

12 May

St. Pancras/Celtic tree month of Saille ends

13 May

Lemuria/Servatius/Celtic tree month of Huath commences

14 May

St. Bonifatius/Runic half-month of Ing commences

The male consort of the Earth Mother goddess Nerthus, Ing is the god of the hearth and his rune, the symbol of light, the firebrand or beacon that spreads its light far and wide. This time of year expresses the energy-potential of summer and its capacity for abundant growth.

15 May

Maia and Mercury/Vesta/Cold Sophie/Ides of May/Goddess month of Maia ends/Egyptian Day

Today is sacred to the month goddess Maia and her son Mercury, and also to Vesta (right), goddess of the hearth and eternal fires. On the Ides of May, the vestal virgins, the ancient Roman priestesses of Vesta, performed a rite intended to regulate the water supply for the coming summer. In southern Germany this is the day of Cold Sophie, when extra-cold weather is expected and needs to be counteracted by appeals to the goddess of fire and warmth.

16 May

St. Brendan the Navigator/Goddess month of Hera commences

The legendary voyages of the Irish Celtic priest, St. Brendan the Navigator, are remembered today. According to some, St. Brendan was the first European to set foot in America.

17 May

Dea Dia

The festival of Dea Dia celebrates the goddess in her aspect as the cosmos, mother to all of us.

18 May

Apollon Day

A day sacred to Apollo, the Greco-Roman god of music, poetry, divination, and sunlight.

19 May

20 May

☽ Mjollnir/☽ Ascension/Egyptian Day

F The Germanic Pagan festival of Mjollnir celebrates the hammer of Thor (right). In medieval times, this day was considered to be a good day for ritual contest, such as trial by combat. Ascension, falling forty days after Easter, marks the completion of this spring cycle of holy days.

21 May

Plato

Plato was born on this day in 429 B.C.E.

22 May

Ragnar Lodbrok

Ragnar Lodbrok was a Viking leader captured by the Northumbrians, then tortured and killed by being thrown into a pit full of venomous snakes. His death song expresses this unwavering faith in the afterlife: "The Disir call me back home, those whom Odin has sent for me from the halls of the lord of hosts. Gladly will I sup ale in the high seat with the gods.

The days of my life are finished. I laugh as I die!" In East Anglia this day is also the last for picking dandelions for wine making.

23 May

Rosalia

The rose festival was celebrated by the Romans in honor of the goddess Flora.

24 May

The Mothers/Hermes Trismegistus

This day is sacred to the Mothers, three goddesses worshiped in Celtic countries as bringers of prosperity and a good harvest. Also the feast day of Hermes Trismegistus, patron of alchemy. At left are two versions of a rope caduceus, the symbol of Hermes.

25 May

Edmund I

The Anglo-Saxon king, Edmund I, was stabbed to death on this day in the year 949 C.E.

26 May

27 May

28 May

29 May

Ambarvalia/Oak Apple Day/Runic half-month of Odal commences

 Ambarvalia was the Roman festival of purification in honor of Ceres and the Dea Dia, involving ritual walking around fields of growing crops to gain divine favor for the plants. In England, the festival became Oak Apple Day, commemorating the escape of Charles II from Cromwell's army by hiding in an oak tree. It is customary to wear oak leaves on this day until midday. The rune Odal signifies ancestral property, the homestead, and all those things that are "one's own."

30 May

Frigg/ ☽ Whitsunday

The holy day of the Norse goddess Frigg, queen of heaven, consort of Odin. Although a major holy day in the Church (signifying the descent of the holy spirit

 to the apostles), in the country this Sunday was also a traditional time for brewing Whitsun ales and for making love bowers and mazes (left).

31 May

JUNE

June is named after the Roman Great Mother goddess Juno, the Greek Hera. The month's name was
originally Junonius. Juno has many attributes, the
chief of which is as the queen of heaven. This at-
tribute is ascribed to Frigg in the Northern Tradition and Mary in the Christian. As ruler of the high
point of the year, the time of the maximum light
and minimum darkness, Juno is the light counterpart of Janus, the ruler of the New Year period.
Because Juno is the divine watcher over the female
sex, the month of June is held to be the most favor-
able for marrying. As Juno Moneta, guardian of money and wealth, the
goddess had a temple dedicated to her on the Capitoline hill in Rome. This
contained the mint where coinage was produced. This theme of wealth
can also be seen in the runic year cycle: the half-month of Feoh, the time
of wealth and abundance, begins on 29 June.

On or about 21 June is the summer solstice, the festival of Midsummer, the Anglo-Saxon Litha and the Alban Hefin of the Druids. The Irish
name for June is Meitheamh, while the Anglo-Saxon was Aerra Litha,
"before Litha." The Franks called June Brachmanoth, "break month,"
while in modern Asatru it is called Fallow. The Hot or Strawberry Moon
is the backwoods' full moon. The month of June is "the door of the year,"
the gateway to the inner realms. The rune Dag that rules the middle of the
month, is the rune of opening, representing the door that excludes bad
things and admits only that which is beneficial. The runic year begins in
June, with Feoh. The Celtic tree-calendar month of Huath—hawthorn—
ends on 9 June to be followed on the 10th by the oak month, Duir. This is
a month of strengthening and consolidation of gains. It can also be said to
represent the "door" of the year, opening to let the sun shine in. Duir has
the sacred color of black. In the goddess calendar, the first twelve days of

June belong to Hera. On 13 June begins the month of Rosea. The precious stone associated with June is the agate, whose traditional rhyme is as follows:

> *Who comes with summer to this earth,*
> *And owes to June her hour of birth.*
> *With ring of Agate on her hand*
> *Can health, wealth and long life command.*

Good weather in "Flaming June" is necessary if there is to be a good harvest. Country weather lore states:

> *If June with bright sun is blessed,*
> *For harvest we will thank the goddess.*

Conversely, it is said that if it rains on 27 June, then it will rain for the next seven weeks. But "A wet June makes a dry September," and "A dripping June brings all things in tune." If swallows fly near the ground in June, it is a sign of coming rain. Bats flying on a June evening are a sign of hot, dry weather the next day.

1 June

Kalends of June/Carna/Syn/Tempestas

K This festival was sacred to Carna, the Roman goddess of doors and locks. She was the protector of family life, equivalent to the Norse goddess Syn, the includer and excluder. Doors and windows should be repaired on this day, which is also the day of the goddess of the storm, Tempestas, who tests them without mercy!

2 June

Mother Earth/ ☽ Mother Shipton's Day

Sacred to Mother Earth in her fecund aspect. Mother Shipton (Ursula Sontheil) was a famous seer in Cambridge, England, and is the patron saint

of women working in laundries. She is honored on the Wednesday immediately after Whitsunday.

3 June

4 June

Socrates/Egyptian Day

  Socrates was born on this day in 470 B.C.E.

5 June

St. Gobnatt

The Irish saint, Gobnatt, is a version of the deity, Domna, patroness of sacred stones and cairns, honored by ritual perambulation. The center of her worship was at Ballyvourney, county Cork, Ireland.

6 June

7 June

Vesta/Nones of June

N The day of the Vesta Aperit, the opening of the sanctuary of the temple of Vesta in Rome.

8 June

Mens/Lindisfarne Day/Egyptian Day

F The old Roman festival of consciousness, personified as the goddess Mens, the mind, is intended to remind us that our consciousness makes us human, and so we should always act consciously. It is celebrated by Odinists as Lindisfarne Day, commemorating the first Viking raid in Britain. This day is also a weather marker:

> *If on the eighth of June it rain,*
> *It foretells a wet harvest, men sain.*

9 June

Vesta/Celtic tree month of Huath ends

The feast day of Vesta, the goddess of the hearth and its fire.

10 June

Celtic tree month of Duir commences/Egyptian Day

The month of the oak, Duir, the most sacred tree of the Druids, during which the summer solstice, the solar high point of the year, takes place.

11 June

Fortuna

A sacred day at the temple of Fortuna in Rome.

12 June

Goddess month of Hera ends

13 June

Athena/Alexander the Great/Goddess month of Rosea commences

The goddess Athena (right), known to the Romans as Minerva, represents the harmonious blending of power and wisdom and is patroness of both the practical and aesthetic arts.

14 June

Vidar/St. Vitus/St. Dogmael/Runic half-month of Dag commences

In modern Asatru, a day sacred to Vidar, son of Odin. According to Viking tradition, leather workers should put aside all of their off-cuts for Vidar's boots, so that the god can combat the demonic wolf, Fenris. The runic letter is a beneficial rune of light, health, prosperity, and openings, signifying the high point of the day and high point of the year, when, in light and warmth, all things are possible. This day is also a weather marker:

If St. Vitus's Day be rainy weather,
It will rain for thirty days together.

15 June

Vestalia/Ides of June

I The Vestalia is the Roman women's festival of first fruits, sacred to the goddess Vesta. It is the day on which the sanctuary of the temple of Vesta was closed (see 7 June).

16 June

17 June

Ludi Piscatari/St. Botolph

The Roman festival of Ludi Piscatari, festival of fishermen, is sacred in England to the East Anglian saint, Botolph, and as such is a day of guardianship. In medieval times, churches dedicated to St. Botolph guarded the gates of ancient English walled cities. His sigil is an Egyptian diamond (above), one of the markers used to this day in navigation.

18 June

19 June

20 June

Iron Skegge

The eve of the summer solstice, marks the martyrdom of Iron Skegge, tortured on the orders of the Norwegian king, Olaf Tryggvason. He died rather than give up his Pagan faith. At right is the Valknut, the knot of the slain, symbol of Odin's martyrs.

21 June

☉ *Summer Solstice: Midsummer, Litha, Alban Hefin, Seventh Station of the Year/All Heras/* ☽ *Islamic New Year*

Midsummer, Druidic festival of Alban Hefin, Anglo-Saxon Litha, is the longest day and seventh station of the year, the time of sanctification. At Stonehenge, the heelstone marks the midsummer sunrise as seen from the center of the stone circle. Since time immemorial, people have acknowledged the rising sun of midsummer. This is also the Day of All Heras in the women's mysteries. Heras are women who have achieved full spiritual communion with the Great Goddess.

22 June

Egyptian Day

23 June

St. John's Eve

St. John's Eve was a traditional time of meditation, awaiting the northernmost sunrise.

24 June

Fortuna/St. John the Baptist/Old Midsummer

A sacred day of the goddess Fortuna, Lady Luck. As St. John the Baptist's Day, it is also the official Midsummer's Day. It is customary to light midsummer bonfires on high points to celebrate the high point of the year and of solar light. Traditional locations for St. John's Day fires are often places where the sun was observed in former times. St. John the Baptist is pictured at right.

25 June

26 June

27 June

Initium Aestatis/Death of Julian the Blessed

Initium Aestatis, the Roman festival of the beginning of summer, celebrates Aestas, the tutelary goddess of summertime. The Roman emperor Julian the Blessed, champion of the Pagan religion, died on this day in the

year 363 C.E. Country
weather lore asserts that
if rain falls on 27 June,
there will be seven weeks
of wet weather.

28 June

Runic New Year's Eve

Final day of the runic year, the last day ruled by
Dag. The eight-pointed sigil is symbolic of
completion.

29 June

Runic New Year/Half-month of Feoh commences/Petosiris/St. Peter

This is an important day in the runic year cycle, marking
the beginning of the first rune, Feoh, sacred to Frey and
Freyja, the lord and lady worshiped in modern Wicca. It is
the half-month of wealth and success. As St. Peter's Day it
is a day of foundations. It also commemorates the Egyptian astrologer and high priest of Thoth, Petosiris of

Hermopolis (c. 300 B.C.E.), whose
tomb became a place of pilgrimage after his death and
canonization. In the traditions
of East Anglia today is the op-
timal day in the year for har-
vesting herbs.

30 June

JULY

July is named after Julius Caesar, who reorganized the previously chaotic Roman calendar with the help of Alexandrian sages to form the Julian calendar. This new calendar was instituted in the year 46 B.C.E., known as the year of confusion after the chaos caused by changing from one calendar to another. The Julian calendar became the main calendar in the West for the next 1600 years. It was current in Britain until 1752, although it was replaced in Catholic countries by the Gregorian calendar in 1582. Some customary days are still kept in the "Old Style," that is, the Julian calendar, rather than the current "New Style" Gregorian one. When the newer calendar was set up, Julius's name remained on the seventh month in commemoration of his work.

As with the modern English name, the Irish name of this month is based on Julius, Iuil. The Anglo-Saxon name for July is Aeftera Litha, "after Litha," acknowledging its position after the summer solstice. An alternative Anglo-Saxon name for the month of July is Maedmonat, "meadow month," because the meadows are at their greatest point of growth in this month. July's Frankish name is related to Hewimanoth, "hay month," a name that is continued in modern Asatru as Haymoon. These month names describe the traditional labor of the month, hay cutting. The full moon this month is the Buck Moon in the American backwoods tradition.

The Celtic tree-calendar month of the oak, Duir, ends on 7 July. The following day sees the beginning of the month of Tinne, the holly tree. This is a month of balance, whose sacred color is dark gray-green. A complementary meaning of Tinne is fire, appropriate for July, the fieriest month of the year. In the goddess calendar, the month of Rosea ends on 10 July. It is followed on 11 July by Kerea.

The birthstone of July is the ruby, whose adage goes:

> *The glowing Ruby shall adorn*
> *Those who in warm July are born.*
> *Then will they be exempt and free*
> *From love's doubt and anxiety.*

Weather lore for July says that rain in the third hour of a July afternoon is the heaviest in the year. July 15 is St. Swithin's Day, a weather marker. A country weather rhyme for July is:

> *A shower of rain in July, when the corn begins to fill,*
> *Is worth a plough of oxen, and all belongs theretill.*
> *In this month is Swithin's Day,*
> *On which, if that rain, men say,*
> *Full forty days after it will*
> *For more or less some rain distil,*
> *Till Swithin's Day is past and gone*
> *There may be hops, or there may be none.*

1 July
Kalends of July

K A weather marker:

> *If July the first be rainy weather,*
> *It will rain for four more weeks together.*

2 July

3 July
Dog Days begin/Loki's Brand

The dog days, ruled by the Dog Star, Sirius, called Loki's Brand in the Northern Tradition, begin today. Traditionally, the hottest part of the year.

4 July

5 July

6 July

Julian the Blessed

The Roman emperor Flavius Claudius Julianus (331–363 C.E.), known as Julian the Blessed, was a learned philosopher in his own right and the restorer of the Pagan religion to the Roman Empire.

7 July

The Consualia/Caprotina/Feriae Ancillarum/ Nones of July/Celtic tree month of Duir ends

N The Roman festival of the Consualia commemorates Consus, the god of harvests, presaging a good harvest later in the month. Today is also the Feriae Ancillarum, the Festival of Handmaids or the maids' day out, when the maids of Rome were beyond the control of their mistresses. Fig trees were venerated on this day, with feasting beneath them in honor of Caprotina, an aspect of the goddess Juno.

8 July

St. Sunniva/Celtic tree month of Tinne commences

 Sometimes observed as the continuation of the Caprotine Nones this is also the feast of St. Sunniva, the medieval version of the Norse solar maiden, Sunna.

9 July

Egyptian Day

10 July

Holda/Hela/Skadi/Lady Godiva/Knut the Reaper/
Goddess month Rosea ends

Holda, Hela, and Skadi are north European goddesses of the shades and the underworld. The
sky-clad Lady Godiva was said to have ridden
through Coventry on this day. Her procession at
Southam, near Coventry, used to include the
images of two goddesses, one the white Holda
and the other the black Hela. Knut the Reaper,
whose symbol is the hay-cutting scythe, is also
worshiped today. The scythe is also the emblem
of the scathing destroyer goddess Skadi, patroness of Scotland and Scandinavia.

11 July

Theano/Goddess month of Kerea commences

Commemorates Theano,
wife of the Greek philosopher Pythagoras, who was a
philosopher in her own right
and sometimes seen as pa-
troness of vegetarianism.

12 July

13 July

14 July

Runic half-month of Ur commences

The half-month of Ur, primal strength, is a time of collective action, when our power as a society can be best applied to projects for the common good. It is a good time for beginnings, for this rune is sacred to the Norn Urda, the primal foundation of things, and to the active principle in the shape of Thor, the hammer-wielding thunder god.

15 July

Ides of July/Olympic New Year/Rowana/St. Swithin/Egyptian Day

The rowan tree goddess, Rowana or Rauni, is patroness of the secret knowledge of the runes. The rowan is the tree of protection and its wood, used in making defensive amulets, is especially effective if cut on this day. St. Swithin's Day is a weather marker. If it rains this day, it is said, then it will rain for the next forty days.

16 July

17 July

18 July

John Dee

Dr. John Dee, English astrologer, alchemist, and mathematician born in 1527.

19 July

Adonia

Today marks the high point of Adonis's six-month presence in the world through the summer half of the year. A sacred drama of the wedding of Adonis (right) and Aphrodite is celebrated on this day.

20 July

21 July

Damo/Egyptian Day

The seeress Damo, venerated today, was the daughter of the Greek sage, Pythagoras. All of the secrets of his philosophy were entrusted to her at his death.

22 July

23 July
Neptunalia and Salacia/Aegir and Ran

The Neptunalia celebrates the divinity of the sea god, Neptune. His wife, Salacia, is goddess of the wide open, salty sea. Inland, she rules over springs of highly mineralized waters. The goddess Sulis, worshiped at the sacred hot springs at Bath, appears to be  an aspect of Salacia. In the north, Neptune and Salacia are equivalent to the Norse god, Aegir, and his consort, Ran.

24 July

25 July
Furrinalia

Furrina was an ancient Italian goddess of springs. This festival is related closely to that of 23 July. Now is the time when a drought may  begin to "bite," and the value of springs is appreciated. A good day to remember our vital reliance on sources of water.

26 July
Sleipnir

Sleipnir is the shamanic steed that can be used to travel to other levels or states of consciousness. The associated Asatru festival commemorates Odin's eight-legged steed, which takes the rider between the three worlds, from the upper one of the gods, Asgard, through our own middle one, Midgard, into the underworld of the shades, Utgard.

27 July

St. Pantaleone

St. Pantaleone, worshiped today, was among other things the patron saint of trousers!

28 July

Domhnach Chrom Dubh

The Irish sacrificial god, Domhnach Chrom Dubh, is connected with the festival of Lammas as is John Barleycorn, personification of grain, who is killed by being cut at this time. At right is Fionn's wheel, a shield with magical formulae that make it a symbol of protection.

29 July

St. Olaf/Thor/Runic half-month of Thorn commences

Northern Tradition honors the god known to the Anglo-Saxons as Thunor and to the Norse as Thor (right). The time of Thorn is one of ascendant powers and

 orderliness. This day also honors the sainted Norwegian king, Olaf, slain around Lammas Day. Its traditional calendar symbol is an axe.

30 July

31 July

Lammas Eve/Loki and Sigyn

Norse trickster god Loki and his consort Sigyn are honored today.

august

August is named after the first Roman emperor, Augustus Caesar (23 September, 63 B.C.E.-29 August, 14 C.E.). The tutelary goddess of August is Demeter or Ceres. According to legend, Demeter left Olympus, abode of the gods, to dwell on Earth. Her beneficent qualities and virtues are most apparent during this month of harvests. The Anglo-Saxon name for it is another descriptive one: Weodmonath, "vegetation month." The Frankish name is Aranmanoth, "corn ears month." To modern Asatru, it is simply the month of Harvest. The full moon this month in the American backwoods tradition is the Sturgeon or Corn Moon. The first day of the month is the cross-quarter day festival of Lammas, the eighth station of the year. Many Pagans call it Lughnassadh, which is the unreformed Irish spelling of the modern Irish name, Lunasa. The Irish name for the day itself is La Lunasa. The ancient Pagan Irish Lughnassadh Assembly describes the themes associated with this festival:

> *Heaven, Earth, Sun, Moon and Sea,*
> *Fruits of Earth and Sea-stuff,*
> *Mouths, ears, eyes, possessions,*
> *Feet, hands, warriors' tongues.*

Lammas is the first harvest of the traditional year, that of grain. This month is sacred to the god of wisdom, Lugh, tutelary deity of London, and Lyons, who is the Celtic parallel of the Norse Odin. The Celtic holly month Tinne ends on 4 August, to be followed by Coll, the hazel month. This is a time of gathering fruitfulness, figuratively in the use of words and divination, giving us creative power and energy. Its sacred color is brown, and its ruling being is the Irish demigod, Fionn MacCumhaill (often anglicized as Finn McCool). The goddess-calendar month of Kerea runs until 8 August, to be followed by the month of Hesperis. In Egypt the fixed Alexandrian calendar has its New Year's Eve on 29 August. This calendar was standardized in the year 30 B.C.E., beginning on this day with the month of Thoth, but it has subsequently succumbed to first the Julian and then the Islamic calendar.

The birthstone of August is the sardonyx, whose adage goes:

> *Wear a Sardonyx or for thee*
> *No conjugal felicity.*
> *Those August born without this stone*
> *'Tis said must live unloved, alone.*

Country weather lore for August links it as follows: "As August, so next February." Also, "A fog in August means a severe winter and plenty of snow." The immediate weather concerns the forthcoming harvest, so of course, "Dry August and warm, doth harvest no harm." A "green sky" above the sunset presages a rainy morning. In this month, moon lore is important too. If a ring or halo appears around the moon, it foretells coming rain. The moon features in another traditional August weather rhyme:

> *Pale moon doth rain, red moon doth blow.*
> *White moon doth neither rain nor snow.*

Of course, the likelihood of snow in August is almost nil.

1 August

Cross-quarter day: Lammas, Lughnassadh, Eighth Station of the Year/ Kalends of August/Egyptian Day

K
F
At this festival of the first harvest, the first corn is cut, baked into a loaf, and offered to the goddess in thanksgiving. Lammas is the eighth and last station of the year, completion, sacred to Odin and Frigg. Celebrants would

ascend the spiral path of the Lammas hill, pictured at left, on their way to Lammas festivities.

2 August

William II Rufus

The anniversary of the death of the second Norman king of England, William II Rufus, killed by an archer in the New Forest in 1100. Many Pagans believe that he, along with other "sacred" kings who died violently on days close to the cross-quarter days, such as Olaf of Norway, were victims of the tradition of sacrificial kingship.

3 August

4 August

Vigil of St. Oswald/Celtic tree month of Tinne ends

Commemorates the Anglo-Saxon king of Northumbria, Oswald, who died in battle in 642 C.E. In the tradition of sacred kingship, his body was dismembered and its dispersed parts became the foci for miracles of healing.

5 August

St. Oswald/Celtic tree month of Coll commences

Coll, the hazel, is symbolic of wisdom and druidry. It signifies the art of regeneration through the use of words, the power of meditation, and—through its use by water dowsers—divination of hidden or lost things.

6 August

Tan

The Tan Hill festival commemorates the personified Celtic holy fire, Teinne or Tan. A festival related to Lammas, it takes place two days after the end of the Celtic tree month of Tinne.

7 August

8 August

Goddess month of Kerea ends

9 August

Goddess month of Hesperis commences

10 August

11 August

12 August

Lights of Isis/St. Clare/William Blake

Ancient Egyptian festival of the Lights of Isis, later became the Christian day of St. Clare. Today is also the anniversary of the death of visionary artist and poet William Blake.

13 August

Hecate/Runic half-month of As commences

Another festival of the goddess Hecate (right). The rune As is sacred to the deities of Asgard: a time of stability, with the divine force obviously at work in the world. This letter corresponds with the ash tree. The world ash, Yggdrasil, is a symbol of continuity in times of change and chaos. The Odinic festival of the runes falls within this half-month (see 25 August).

14 August

15 August

The Great Mother Goddess/Assumption of the Virgin Mary/Dog Days end

Day of St. Mary, the continuation of the Great Mother goddess in her fertile aspect, when she is invoked to ensure a good vintage:

> *On St. Mary's Day, sunshine*
> *Brings much good wine.*

This is the Christian festival of the Assumption of the Virgin Mary. It also marks the end of the dog days, the hottest period of the year. At right is Arianrod, a Celtic mother goddess.

16 August

17 August

Odin's Ordeal (1)

The first day of Odin's ordeal on the world tree Yggdrasil, leading to the discovery of the runes. According to the *Edda*, Odin hung on

the tree for nine days and nights. This is commemorated from 17 August to 25 August, the final day being the festival of the Discovery of the Runes, when Odin fell "screaming" from the tree, having gained the knowledge.

18 August

Odin's Ordeal (2)

19 August

Odin's Ordeal (3)/The Rustic Vinalia/Egyptian Day

 Roman festival of the Rustic Vinalia is a day of offering to the ripening grapes. This is a festival of the goddess Venus (right), in her aspect as guardian of gardens, olive groves, and vineyards.

20 August

Odin's Ordeal (4)/Egyptian Day

21 August

Odin's Ordeal (5)

22 August

Odin's Ordeal (6)/Aedesia

The fifth century Neoplatonic philosopher Aedesia is remembered today.

23 August

Odin's Ordeal (7)/Nemesea/Vertumnalia/
Vulcan and the Nymphs

Day of the Nemesea, the celebration of the Greek goddess Nemesis (right), defender of the relics and memory of the dead from insult and injury. Day of the Vertumnalia, held in celebration of Vertumnus (left), Roman god of the change of the seasons and the transformation of flowers into fruits. It is

also the festival of Vulcan (left) and the Nymphs.

24 August

Odin's Ordeal (8)/Mania (first day)/St. Bartholomew

The Mania is a Roman festival acknowledging the manes, deified spirits of the ancestors. St. Bartholomew's (or Bartlemy's) Day is a weather marker:

> *If Bartlemy's Day be fair and clear,*
> *Hope for a prosperous autumn this year.*

London's Bartholomew Fair was a continuation of the Roman festival of the Mania.

25 August

Ops/Odin's Ordeal (9)/Discovery of the Runes

The Italian earth goddess of sowing and reaping, Ops (right), is remembered in the Opiconsivia, a ceremony at which only vestal virgins were present. Her worshipers always sat on the earth.

26 August

Ilmatar

Ilmatar is a Finnish goddess, known as the Water Mother. According to tradition this goddess is the creator of the world. Pictured at right is a traditional calendrical sigil for this day.

27 August

Nativity of Isis

28 August

Nativity of Nephthys

Nephthys is the Egyptian equivalent of Aphrodite.

29 August

Urda/Nativity of Hathor/Augustus/Runic half-month of Rad commences/ Egyptian Day

 Urda is the oldest of the three Norns (fates) and represents "that which was." She is honored today. The deified Roman emperor,

Augustus, after whom the month is named, is remembered on this, the day of his death. The Egyptians celebrated the nativity of the goddess Hathor (left) on this day. The Runic half-month of Rad denotes the channeling of energies in the correct manner to produce the desired results.

30 August

Alexandrian New Year/Charisteria

The first day of the month of Thoth, the New Year's Day of the fixed Greco-Egyptian calendar of Alexandria. It is the old Roman festival of thanksgiving, the Charisteria. Thoth is pictured at right.

31 August

septembeR

September is so called because it was the seventh month of the old Roman calendar. The names of the three following months, October, November, and December, also bear old Roman month numbers, eight, nine, and ten, respectively. The goddess Pomona, patroness of fruit and fruit-bearing trees, is the ruling deity of the month of September. This is the Irish month of Mean Fomhair. Its Anglo-Saxon name was Haligmonath, "holy month." This is rather paradoxical, as the first part of the month has significantly fewer sacred festivals than most other months do. To the Franks it was Witumanoth, "wood month," in which wood was gathered in advance of the approaching winter. To modern Asatru, it is the month of Shedding. The backwoods' moon of September is the Harvest Moon.

The Celtic tree-calendar month of Coll ends on 1 September. From 2 September until 29 September is the vine month of Muin, sacred to the god Lugh, with "variegated" colors. Gort begins on 30 September. This is the ivy month, sacred to the goddess Brigid, with the color of sky blue. The month of Gort is a time for the development of the self, a period when one can see beyond the everyday world to that which lies within and beyond. It symbolizes the spiral ascent of the spirit from the plane of Abred (the material world) to Gwynvyd (the world of enlightenment). The goddess calendar month of Hesperis runs until 5 September, giving way to the month of Mala on 6 September.

The stone for September is the sapphire:

A maiden born when rustling leaves
Are blowing in the September breeze,

A Sapphire on her brow should bind,
'Twill cure diseases of the mind.

September is most notable for containing the autumnal equinox, the Mabon of Celtic tradition, the Alban Elfed of the Druids, and the Winter Finding of the Norse. Movable days that occur in September (or October) include the Jewish New Year (Rosh Hashanah), Yom Kippur, and Simhat Torah. Weather lore for September says that the month is one of extremes. It is able to either dry up wells or break down bridges. "If it be fair on the first day of September, it will remain so at least to the beginning of October." It is said in East Anglian lore that there are three very windy days during the mid-September Barleysel (barley harvest). These are the equinoctial storms associated with the period. "September blow soft, till the fruit's in the loft" is the spell against potential wind-borne disaster during the fruit harvest of this month.

1 September

Kalends of September/St. Giles/Celtic tree month of Coll ends

K Wounded in the leg by an arrow while protecting a stag that the king of Provence was trying to shoot, Giles became patron of the disabled, and was prayed to for cures. Many hospitals were dedicated to him, all later closed by Henry VIII, as were the Catholic monasteries and fairs at Oxford and Winchester. At right is a medieval tradesman's mark from Bohemia, dedicated to St. Giles.

2 September

Celtic tree month of Muin commences/St. Sulien/Egyptian Day

 This is harvest time when the raw materials of life, both physical and spiritual, are collected for processing into something higher. The release of prophetic powers is promised by the month of Muin, which is sacred to the god Lugh, Celtic deity of the light of the intellect and spiritual illumination.

3 September

4 September

Egyptian Day

5 September

Nones of September/Goddess month of Hesperis ends

6 September

Goddess month of Mala commences/Egyptian Day

7 September

Egyptian Day

8 September

Mary, the Blessed Virgin

The feast of the nativity of Mary. The weather today is said to determine that of the following four weeks.

9 September

Asclepigenia/Horned Dance at Abbots Bromley

The day on which Asclepigenia, a priestess of the Greek Eleusinian Mysteries, is commemorated. Traditionally, the Horn Dance at Abbots Bromley is held two weeks before the equinox when dancers carry ancient reindeer horns. This custom, now and at the New Year, is a Pagan tradition representing the Horned One, who is most commonly called Cernunnos. This day is also a weather marker. If the weather is fine today, it will continue fine for another forty days.

10 September

Egyptian Day

11 September

12 September

13 September

Ides of September/Lectisternia/Runic half-month of Ken commences

The Roman festival of the Lectisternia was held in honor of Jupiter, Juno, and Minerva. The rune Ken represents the flaming torch within the royal hall, the time of the creative fire—the forge where natural materials are transmuted by the actions of the human will into a mystical third, an artefact that could not otherwise come into being. The positive aspects of sexuality immanent in the goddess Freyja and the god Frey come into play at this time.

14 September

Feast of Lights

This ancient Egyptian ceremony involved offerings of light burning all night before images of the gods and the tombs of the dead.

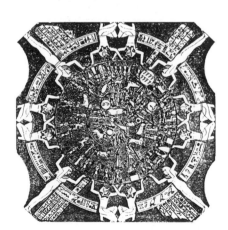

15 September

16 September

☽ *Rosh Hashanah*

Rosh Hashanah, the Jewish New Year, is celebrated.

17 September

18 September

Egyptian Day

19 September

Fast of Thoth

In the Alexandrian calendar this was a day-long fast in honor of Thoth, Egyptian god of wisdom and magic.

20 September

Alexander

Alexander the Great, deified after his death, was born accompanied by great omens on this day in 356 B.C.E.

21 September

St. Matthew/Feast of the Divine Life/Raud the Strong/Egyptian Day

 St. Matthew's Day is a weather marker associated with the grape harvest:

> *Matthew's Day, bright and clear,*
> *Brings good wine in the next year.*

The Egyptian feast of the Divine Life is dedicated to the threefold god-dess—the mother (creatrix of all things), the daughter (renewer), and the

dark mother (the absolute). The martyrdom of Raud the Strong by the Norwegian king, Olaf Tryggvason, is also commemorated on the eve of the autumnal equinox. Raud died under hideous tortures rather than abjure his faith in the old gods of the North.

22 September

23 September

☉ *Autumnal Equinox: Mabon, Alban Elfed, Winter Finding, Second Station of the Year/Carpo/Carman/Egyptian Day*

A time when darkness overtakes light, and nights grow longer than days. It marks the second station of the year. It is the time of calling, ripening of the harvest, a prelude to awakening at Samhain. If it is warm at the autumnal equinox, the season should be fine. The goddesses Carpo and Carman are deities of autumn and poetry, respectively.

24 September

25 September

☽ *Yom Kippur*

Yom Kippur, the Day of Atonement, is a day of fasting.

26 September

27 September

28 September

Runic half-month of Gyfu commences

Gyfu represents the unity that a gift brings between the donor and recipient. It is a time of unification, both between the members of society and the human and the divine.

29 September

Michaelmas/Gwynn ap Nudd/Heimdall/ Celtic tree month of Muin ends

St. Michael is chief of the angels in the Christian tradition, a warrior as well as a master of heaven. Equivalent figures celebrated on the same day are the Celtic Gwynn ap Nudd, lord of the underworld and the faerie kingdom, whose sacred mountain is Glastonbury Tor, and the Norse Heimdall (right), orderer of society, watcher of the gods,

and captain of the 432,000 Einheriar, the chosen warriors who defend Valhalla. September 29 is a weather marker: "Harvest comes as long before Michaelmas as dog roses bloom before Midsummer."

Curious ritual biscuits in the form of a man riding a goose, known as Taffy on a Goose, were sold on this day in Norwich, Norfolk, England, until the outbreak of World War II in 1939.

30 September

Medetrinalia/Celtic tree month of Gort commences

Offerings of fruit are made on this day to Medetrina, the Roman goddess of medicines.

OCTOBER

October, the eighth month of the old Roman calendar, is sacred to the goddess Astraea. She was the
daughter of Zeus and Themis and lived among humans during the Golden Age. But when civilization
began to degenerate, she withdrew to the upperworld.
The myth of the loss of the Golden Age is appropriate for that time of year when the chills of autumn
tell us that the golden days of summer are past and
that winter is drawing near. The autumn leaves turn
to gold and fall during this month, echoing Astraea's
departure from the earth.

In the Celtic tree calendar, October begins in the ivy month, Gort,
which runs until 27 October. The reed month, Noetal follows. This is
sacred to the fertility sprite Robin Goodfellow, and has the color of grass-
green. It is a time of direct, penetrating vision, the gaining of knowledge
and the capability of discovering order in the unknown. Solar and lunar
forces are said to be in unison during this tree month. October 28 is also
the first day of the Runic half-month of Hagal, a time of transformation.
This rune also symbolizes an underlying orderliness of all things, without
which there would be chaos and nonexistence.

October is the Irish month of Deireadh Fomhair. Its Anglo-Saxon
name, Winterfelleth, means "winter is coming." Its Frankish name,
Windurmanoth, "vintage month," refers to the wine harvest. The American backwoods tradition calls the October full moon the Hunter's Moon,
and the Asatru name for the month is Hunting.

The goddess calendar month of Mala expires on 2 October. It is
followed by the month dedicated to the Egyptian goddess Hathor, ending
on the 30th. The final day of October, Halloween or November Eve, is the
first day of the month ruled by the goddess Samhain. This is the Irish

name of the month of November, and this goddess is the personification of the virtues of this time of year.

The festival of Samhain begins at sunset on 31 October, the New Year of the Celtic tradition. Traditionally, this is the time of the first frosts and the final harvest. At this festival, the herds were brought back from the upland fields into the warmth of the lowland home pastures and cattle sheds. Old and surplus stock was slaughtered and salted or smoked for use during the forthcoming winter. Some of the meat was consumed at the great feast of Samhain, washed down with the new harvest's beer or wine.

The birthstone of October is the opal, which is seen as an averter of otherwise painful times, as the adage tells us:

> *October's child is born for woe,*
> *And life's vicissitudes must know:*
> *But lay an Opal on her breast,*
> *And hope will lull those woes to rest.*

The weather lore of October states that the more bright red berries (haws and hips) that can be seen in the hedgerows, the more frost and snow there will be in the forthcoming winter. But the month itself need not be cold and wintry. October is noted for its second summer in many lands of the Northern Hemisphere. In Sweden, it is called St. Bridget's summer. In the United States, it is Indian summer, while in Italy it is the summer of St. Teresa; in Germany and Switzerland, it is the summer of St. Gall; and in England, St. Luke's summer. The feast days of all of these saints fall in October. Movable feasts in October include the Asatru Winter Saturday and Sunday. A noted day for rain is 28 October, the day of Fyribod. Much rain in October is said to correspond with much rain in December, while a warm October makes a cold February. If the weather is bad, however, the opposite should be true:

> *If October bring much frost and wind,*
> *Then are January and February mild.*

October is also the month for fertilizing the fields for the next year's growing season:

> *In October dung your field,*
> *And your land its wealth shall yield.*

1 October

Kalends of October/Fides

K Fides was the personification of faithfulness, worshiped as a goddess in Rome.

2 October

Goddess month of Mala ends/Holy Guardian Angels

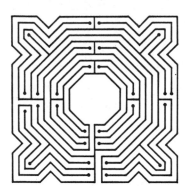

Whether as guardian angels, sprites, or spirits many believe in something that protects each of us from ill. The four-cornered labyrinth is a sigil of guardianship.

3 October

Dionysus/St. Dionysius/Goddess month of Hathor commences

The Grecian divinity Dionysus (and Roman Bacchus) was god of wine and revelry—so this is a time of celebration after the harvest. Old and new wine are mixed together, and the goddess Medetrina is also invoked: "Wine new and old I drink, to cure me of illnesses new and old." St. Dionysius is a Christianized form of the Pagan god.

4 October

Egyptian Day

5 October

Mania

On the second day of the Mania, the Mundus, the passage to the underworld, was believed to be open, allowing the passage of spirits up into our middle world, and the journeys of *shamans* down into the underworld and back. It is a festival when departed ancestors are remembered.

6 October

Egyptian Day

7 October

Nones of October/Pallas Athena/Victoria/Our Lady of Victories

N Pallas Athena (right), patroness of Athens, was later worshiped in Rome as the goddess Victoria, the divine personification of success and triumph. In the Christian era she was transmuted into St. Victoria, or Our Lady of Victories. With the fashion for triumphal architecture, her image was placed on top of ceremonial arches, such as Marble Arch in London and the Brandenburg Gate in Berlin.

8 October

☽ *Simhat Torah*

The Jewish celebration of Simhat Torah, the Rejoicing of the Law, marks the end of the year's cycle of readings from the Torah.

9 October

Felicitas

Felicitas, Roman goddess of good luck and joy, is celebrated today.

10 October

11 October

Vinalia

The Roman Bacchanalian festival of Vinalia was a harvest thanksgiving, at which the new wine was tested. In modern times, this can be taken as the excuse for a party!

12 October

Fortuna Redux

Fortuna Redux, the Roman goddess of successful journeys and safe returns, is worshiped today.

13 October

Fontinalia/Runic half-month of Wyn commences

Fontinalia was a Roman festival at which fountains, that is, holy wells and springs, were venerated. Wyn literally means joy, the rune being the shape of a weather vane. The mystery of harmony within a disharmonious world is now manifest. Wyn stands for the creation of harmony within the given conditions of the present.

14 October

Winter's Day/Vinternatsblót

Winter's Day marks the beginning of the winter season in the old northern European calendar. Long-distance sailing and other summer activities also stopped on this day, as preparations for the winter took priority.

15 October

Ides of October

I In ancient Rome, the tradition of Winter's Day was held a day later than in the north. Here, the season of combat ended, and weapons were put away until the following year.

16 October

Egyptian Day

17 October

St. Audrey/Hengest

St. Audrey's Day is the date of the famous fair at St. Ives in Huntingdonshire, where St. Audrey's trinkets ("tawdry" jewelery) were sold. It is also the Asatru festival of Hengest, which commemorates the Anglo-Saxon settlement of eastern Britain in the fifth century under the generals Hengest and Horsa. At right is Tyr, the Anglo-Saxon god of battlefields.

18 October

Pandrosos

The Greek goddess Pandrosos was known as the all-bedewing or all-refreshing one. She was the deified first priestess of Minerva. Today is the final chance in the year for really good weather, the St. Luke's summer of English tradition.

19 October

20 October

21 October

22 October

23 October

) *Winter Saturday*

This two-day Asatru festival commemorates the changeover to the winter half of the year.

24 October

) *Winter Sunday/Egyptian Day*

 Winter Sunday is the second day of the Asatru observance.

25 October

Dioscuri/Sts. Crispin and Crispinian

The feast of Saints Crispin and Crispinianus was immortalized by Shakespeare in *Henry V*, in the king's speech on the eve of the battle of Agincourt, fought on this day in 1415. These twin saints, patrons of shoemakers, are the continuation of the Dioscuri, Castor and Pollux, sons of Zeus.

Now shoemakers will have a frisken,
All in honour of St. Crispin.

In honor of the Dioscuri, at left is a two-person labyrinth.

26 October

27 October

Celtic tree month of Gort ends

28 October

Fyribod/Runic half-month of Hagal and Celtic tree month of Ngetal commence

The festival of Fyribod, or Forebode, is a marker of winter and bad weather. The runic half-month of Hagal, the transformative hailstone, is a time to undergo the changes leading up to winter. The Celtic tree month of Ngetal, the reed, is symbolic of measurement (as a metewand) and of record (as the reed pen). A time of introspection, analysis, seeking, and finding order.

29 October

30 October

Goddess month of Hathor ends

31 October

Samhain Eve/Halloween/Goddess month of Samhain commences

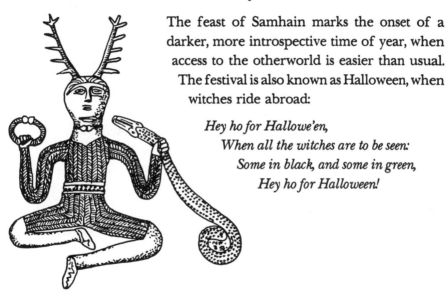

The feast of Samhain marks the onset of a darker, more introspective time of year, when access to the otherworld is easier than usual. The festival is also known as Halloween, when witches ride abroad:

Hey ho for Hallowe'en,
When all the witches are to be seen:
Some in black, and some in green,
Hey ho for Halloween!

NOVEMBER

In the natural year, November is the first month of
the winter quarter. This commences at the festival of
Samhain/All Saints, the first day of the month. In
Celtic tradition, the beginning of the winter quarter
also marked the beginning of the year. Samhain
(pronounced sow-ain) was the first day of the old
Celtic year. In Irish, the name of the day itself, La
Shamhna, is given to the whole month. Although it
is now the eleventh month, November takes its name
from being the original ninth month of the Roman
calendar. But wherever it is placed in the year circle,
this is a month of endings and beginnings. The quarter starting now is
under the guardianship of the Cailleach (the veiled woman), the old
woman goddess. Until Yuletide, this is a time of increasing darkness, the
apparent decline of the living world. It is the time when the link is strong
between the world of the living and the underworld of the dead. As the
third station of the year, it is the time of awakening and letting go, when
the seed falls to earth from its mother plant.

   The Anglo-Saxon name for November was Blotmonath, the month
of sacrifice, the time for killing the livestock that could not be kept
through the winter months. In the Frankish tradition, it was Herbistmanoth,
"harvest month," also referring to the third harvest of animals. Adherents
of Asatru call November Fogmoon, after the most common weather of
the month. This is the Beaver Moon of the American backwoods tradition.

   The Celtic tree-calendar month of Ngetal occupies most of November, ending on the 24th. It is followed by Ruis, the elder month. The elder
is the tree of timelessness in which youth and age, life and death, are in
balance. It is sacred to the Mothers, the three goddesses that personify the
triple goddess of girl, mother, and old woman, particularly in her third
aspect. Its sacred color is red.

Almost all of the month is coincident with the goddess-calendar month of Samhain, the feminine personification of the November cross-quarter day. This goddess is an aspect of the Cailleach. Her month expires at midnight on 27 November, to be followed by the month of Astraea. The ancient Egyptian festival of Isis, the Isia, which reenacted the dismemberment and restoration of Osiris, was held from 1-3 November, coinciding with the Samhain of northern Europe. Apart from the festival of Samhain, November contains Old November Day, otherwise known as Martinmas or Hollantide. This festival, 11 November, once marked the New Year in the Isle of Man. This is the modern Asatru festival of the Einherjar, the heroes who guard the gods. St. Martin's Day is a predictive weather marker. Fine weather on this day is known as St. Martin's summer.

> *If ducks do slide at Hollantide,*
> *At Christmas they will swim.*
> *If ducks do swim at Hollantide,*
> *At Christmas they will slide.*
> *Winter is on his way*
> *At St. Martin's Day.*

The feast day of Wayland, commemorated under the guise of St. Clement, patron saint of smiths, falls on 23 November. The chains binding the demons of the underworld should now be hammered to keep them strong!

The topaz is the jewel of November. It is the emblem of true friendship. The first half of the month is ruled by the rune Hagal, the icy hailstone rune of transformation, connected with the underworld goddess Hela, and the Norn of past times, Urda. From 13 November, the rune Nyd rules. This is the rune of necessity, urging us to accomplish the tasks we need to fulfill before the coming wintertime renders them impossible. At the end of November, the runic half-month of Is—ice—comes into play. This is a time of restricted activity, as the days grow shorter toward the solstice and the weather worsens.

1 November

*Cross-quarter day: Samhain, Festival of the Dead, Third Station of the Year/
Kalends of November/All Saints/Isia*

The third station of the year, awakening, is a time of letting go, when the seed falls to Earth. Samhain is the beginning of winter in the natural year. All Saints' Day is the first day of the two-day Christian commemoration of the dead elevated to sainthood. As a continuation of Samhain, the Eve of All Souls' Day begins at sunset when it is customary to light the bonfires known as *tinley* fires (*teanlas* or *tindles*). The theme of this week is memory of the dead, communication with the underworld, and purification for the future.

2 November

Isia (2)/All Souls

All Souls' Day commemorates departed spirits not elevated to sainthood.

Before becoming a church festival in 998 C.E., it was marked with celebrations from the festival of Woden (Odin) as god of the dead: parading the Hodening wild horse and other guising including mummers' plays enacting the mysteries of life, death, and rebirth. Ceremonial soulcakes were cooked and eaten on this day.

3 November

Isia (3)/St. Malachy

The medieval Irish prophet St. Malachy, the "Irish Nostradamus," is commemorated today. In Celtic tradition, this is the day for starting new enterprises and the day the cattle are taken from the hills to the lowlands for wintertime.

4 November

5 November

Nones of November/Guy Fawkes Night/Egyptian Day

 Guy Fawkes Night, celebrated by the burning in effigy of a would-be regicide, continues the earlier tradition of burning effigies of the evil spirits of the past old year. By cremating them, along with outworn hurts and grievances, the new year may be faced in a purer way, free of unnecessary and unhelpful psychic leftovers.

6 November

St. Leonard/Egyptian Day

St. Leonard, known for dragon slaying, is commemorated today. He is the guardian spirit of St. Leonard's forest in Sussex, England.

7 November

8 November

Mania/Gwynn ap Nudd

The Roman festival of the Mania commemorates the Manes, spirits of the underworld. A day when the lower worlds are accessible. In Celtic tradition, Gwynn ap Nudd (Light, son of Darkness), lord of the faerie kingdom, permits the door to be opened for a day. His abode is Glastonbury Tor, one of the ancient holy mountains of Britain, an entrance to the lower world.

9 November

Helena/Quatuor Coronati

Helena, deified wife of Emperor Julian the Blessed, is commemorated today. It is also the feast of the Four Crowned Martyrs, held in great regard by Freemasons.

10 November

Nincnevin (Diana)/Reason/Old November Eve/Egyptian Day

The Scots Pagan festival of Nincnevin (Martinmas Eve) honors an aspect of Diana, right, who rides with her entourage in the night hours of 9-10 November. During the French Revolution, the goddess of Reason was celebrated in the cathedral of Notre Dame in Paris, which was converted into a temple of philosophy.

11 November

Old November Day/Martinmas/Einherjar

This day marks the full onset of winter. Hiring fairs used to take place today. In Asatru, it is the festival of the Einherjar, the 432,000 spiritual warriors who guard the gods. In Ireland, it is the day of the Lunantishees, spirits that guard the holy blackthorn trees.

12 November

13 November

Feronia/Juno, Minerva, and Jupiter/Runic half-month of Nyd commences

At the Roman festival of Feronia the goddess of this name was worshiped along with Juno, Minerva, and Jupiter, the three Capitoline deities. The runic period of Nyd is a time to prepare for winter.

14 November

Moccas/St. Dubricius

The Celtic saint, Dubricius, is reputed to have been the priest who crowned King Arthur. His legend is associated with the Celtic pig goddess Moccas.

15 November

Egyptian Day

16 November

St. Edmund of East Anglia/Hecate Night

St. Edmund, king of East Anglia, was killed by Danish archers and then beheaded. In the tradition of Saxon magic kingship, his severed head was guarded by a wolf until it and his body were recovered and later buried at St. Edmundsbury, Bury St. Edmunds, in Suffolk, a sacred place of pilgrimage. Sunset marks the beginning of Hecate Night, when the threefold goddess of Wicca (Perseis) is celebrated.

17 November

18 November

19 November

20 November

Praetextatus and Paulina

Praetextatus and Paulina, guardians of the Eleusinian mysteries, are commemorated today. In 364 c.e., they resisted the order of Christian emperor Valentinian to suppress these Greek Pagan mysteries. They continued to allow the entire rite to be performed in the traditional way. At right is Demeter, the presiding goddess of the mysteries.

21 November

22 November

Ydalir/Artemis Calliste/St. Cecilia

 In the Northern Tradition, this is Ydalir, the Valley of the Yews, under the rulership of the wintertime god of skiing and archery, Ullr. Today is celebrated by all music lovers as St. Cecilia's Day. She (right) is patroness of music, an aspect of the goddess Artemis Calliste, the Lily of Heaven. At left is Ul, the rune of healing.

23 November

St. Clement/Wayland

St. Clement's Day marks the first day of winter in the Julian calendar. As patron saint of blacksmiths and metalworkers, Clement is an aspect of the Saxon and Norse godling Wayland the Smith. At the annual blacksmith's feast held at Burwash, Sussex, Old Clem was said to stand protectively above the tavern door.

24 November

Celtic tree month of Ngetal ends

25 November

*Persephone/Proserpina/Kore/St. Catherine/Womens'
Merrymaking Day/Celtic tree month of Ruis commences*

Commemorates the wheel goddess of the underworld, known variously as Persephone (right), Proserpina,

Kore, Arianrod, and Catherine—Queen of the Shades, ruler of the souls of the dead. It was formerly known as Women's Merrymaking Day, a festival of the celebration of women's mysteries.

26 November

Paracelsus

The Swiss alchemist was born on this day in 1493.

27 November

Goddess month of Cailleach ends

28 November

Runic half-month of Is and goddess month of Astraea commence

The runic half-month of Is, literally "ice," is a static period: a time of the cessation of flow and enforced rest.

29 November

Sons of Saturn/St. Saturnius/Egyptian Day

 One of the festivals of the sons of Saturn, in their saintly guise as St. Saturnius. Saturnius, son of Saturn, is the surname of the

gods Jupiter, Neptune, and Pluto, who are commemorated on this day.

30 November

St. Andrew/Egyptian Day

F The saint worshiped today as St. Andrew is a version of the divinity known as Andros, the Man, personification of manhood and the principle of virility, seen as an aspect of Dionysus (right). This is the patronal day of Scotland, whose matronal goddess is Skadi, the Scathing One.

DECEMBER

December is named after the tenth month of the Roman calendar and the middle goddess of the Three Fates, Decima, she who personifies the present. The Roman goddess Vesta, patroness of fire, an archetypal symbol of the eternal present, was also said to rule this month. December's Anglo-Saxon name was Aerra Geola, "the month before Yule." Another version was Wintermonat, "winter month." Because of its unusually large number of sacred festivals, the Frankish tradition called it Heilagmanoth, "holy month," but modern Asatru does not refer to the Yule/Christmas tradition, preferring Wolfmoon. The Irish name of December is Mi na Nollag, Christmas month. The December full moon is the backwoods' Cold or Hunting Moon. The Celtic tree month of Ruis runs until 22 December, when it gives way to the intercalary day of 23 December. The elder month signifies the paradox of a time of timelessness, youth in old age and old age in youthfulness, life in death and death in life. It is the end of the year's cycle and the herald of a new beginning. Change is linked to creativity in the month of Ruis. It is followed by the single blank day in the Celtic calendar known as "the secret of the unhewn stone."

From 24 December, the month of Beth begins. Beth is the first letter of the Celtic ogham alphabet, signifying the birch, sacred to the Great Mother goddess and the prime tree of the tree alphabet, representing new beginnings, purification, and the expulsion of all bad thoughts and influences. The goddess calendar month of Astraea runs until 25 December, Yule Day. It is followed by the month of Hestia, which spans the New Year, ending on 22 January.

The major festival of December is the winter solstice, also called Yule, Alban Arthuan, and Midwinter. The birth of many solar saviors and dying gods is celebrated at this time, usually on 25 December. These saviors include Osiris, the Syrian Baal, Attis, Adonis, Helios, Apollo, Dionysus, Mithras, Jesus, Balder, and Frey. In the Roman tradition 25 December was Dies Natalis Solis Invicti, the Day of the Birth of the Undefeated Sun. All of these deities were given similar titles: the Light of the World, Sun of Righteousness, and Savior. The festival of Christmas is a wonderful amalgam of many religious traditions, ancient and modern, Pagan, Zoroastrian, Jewish, Mithraic, and Christian.

December 31 is the Scottish New Year's festival of Hogmanay. Its name commemorates the solar divinity Hogmagog. As Gogmagog, this solar giant was formerly a chalk-cut hill figure at Wandlebury, close to Cambridge, while, divided into two giants, Gog and Magog, he is the spiritual guardian of the city of London. The traditional Hogmanay ceremonies involved dressing in the hides of cattle and running around the village, being hit by sticks. Hogmanay festivities include the lighting of bonfires, rolling blazing tar barrels, and tossing blazing torches. In former times, animal hide was wrapped around sticks and ignited, producing a smoke that was said to be effective against evil sprites. The talismanic smoking stick itself was known as a Hogmanay. Hogmanay has its own customary goods: bannocks, oarsmen, shortbread, black buns, and ankersocks (gingerbread loaves made with rye meal). In former times, the shamanic tradition of dressing in animal skins, and often wearing horns or antlers upon the head, was customary on New Year's Eve. At the moment of New Year, the doors and windows of the house were opened to let out the old year and to let the new year in. Household utensils were rattled and banged, to drive away any remaining psychic vestiges of the old year. In Wales, this is said to be done in order to drive away the Cwn Annwn, the phantom black dogs of the underworld that pass through the air on New Year's Eve. The birthstone of December is the turquoise:

If cold December gave you birth,
The month of ice and snow and mirth,
Place on your hand a Turquoise blue,
Success will bless whatever you do.

Traditional weather lore for December states that if it rains during the twelve days after Christmas, then the coming year will also be wet. An old Highland Scottish saying uses the wind direction on the last day of the year to predict the coming weather:

If New Year's Eve night and wind blow south,
It betokeneth warmth and growth;
If west, much fish in the sea;
If north, much cold and storms there will be.
If east, the trees will bear much fruit;
If north-east, flee it, man and brute.

Christmas Day is a major weather marker, with the following traditional adages linking it to Eastertide:

A warm Christmas, a cold Easter;
A green Christmas, a white Easter;
Christmas in snow, Easter in wind;

Snow at Christmas brings a good hay crop next year;
A light Christmas, a heavy sheaf;
Christmas wet, empty granary and barrel;

If the sun shines through the apple trees on Christmas day,
there will be a fine crop on the following year;
If there is wind on Christmas day, there will be much fruit.

1 December

Kalends of December/Poseidon

K Festival of Poseidon, Greek god of the sea and of rebirth.

2 December

3 December

Bona Dea

Roman festival of Bona Dea, the Good Goddess.

4 December

Pallas Athena/St. Barbara

St. Barbara's veneration was suppressed by the Roman Catholic church, along with St. George and St. Christopher, in 1969. She is patroness of Santa Barbara
in California, protects against lightning strikes, and has been identified with Pallas Athena, goddess of wisdom and of the useful and elegant arts.

5 December

Eve of St. Nicholas/Nones of December

N In former times, on the Eve of St. Nicholas, children put out carrots, hay, and straw, supposedly for his horse, to be exchanged for presents in the night.

6 December

Thor/St. Nicholas/Santa Claus/Egyptian Day

F The Gnostic followers of St.
Nicholas, the Nicolaites, taught
that the only way to salvation
lay through frequent sexual inter-
course. In northern Europe, St. Nicholas absorbed Pagan attributes from
Woden (Odin), chief of the wild hunt,
who rides through the sky with reindeer and forty-two supernatural hunts-
men. Since the Reformation, this saint has become merged with the Father
Christmas of Yuletide. The modern Santa Claus also has elements of Thor
(above), traditionally depicted riding a goat and carrying a wassail bowl.

7 December

Egyptian Day

F

8 December

Astraea

A day sacred to Astraea, a Greek
goddess of justice.

9 December

☽ *Hanukkah/Egyptian Day*

F The Jewish festival of Hanukkah begins today.

10 December

Lux Mundi/Liberty

This French festival coincides with the older Roman one known as Lux Mundi, the Light of the World, and epithet of the goddess Liberty, whose burning torch of hope shines even in the darkest hour. Her statue graces the harbor of New York City.

11 December

Egyptian Day

12 December

13 December

Ides of December/St. Lucy/Little Yule/Runic half-month of Jara commences

St. Lucy's Day, or Little Yule, is a festival of lights. Jara signifies the completion of natural cycles, such as fruition, and has a more transcendent meaning of mystic marriage between the earth and cosmos.

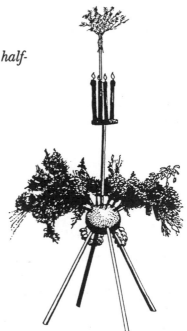

14 December

Nostradamus

Nostradamus, the great French
seer, is remembered today.

15 December

Alcyone/Halcyon Days commence/Egyptian Day

F The Greek goddess Alcyone was symbolized by the kingfisher. Her feast
day marks the beginning of the hal-
cyon days, seven before and seven after the
winter solstice. In ancient Greece, these were
days when the sea was smooth, a time of peace
when the kingfisher could hatch her egg.

16 December

Sapientia/Sophia

The festival of the goddess of wisdom Sapientia, or Sophia, immediately
precedes the major period of license during the year, when wisdom may
not be the ruling quality.

17 December

Saturn/Ops/First day of Saturnalia

The Roman festival of Saturnalia ran
for seven days and was known for its
extravagant decadence. Slaves were al-
lowed to meet their masters on equal
terms. In this season of goodwill to all,

the greeting was "Bona Saturnalia!" The modern celebration of Christmas is a continuation of this midwinter festivity.

18 December

Egyptian Day

19 December

20 December

The Mother Night

The Mother Night is the Odinist festival of midwinter. Dreams on this night are believed to foretell events in the upcoming year.

21 December

☉ *Winter Solstice: Yule, Midwinter, Alban Arthuan, Fourth Station of the Year/St. Thomas*

The Druidic Alban Arthuan, and Christian St. Thomas's Day, when the poor are traditionally given money or presents. In former times the needy could ask for money, a practice known as "thomasing" or "mumping." The fourth station of the year signifies enlightenment, when the light is reborn within the womb of darkness.

22 December

Celtic tree month of Ruis ends/Egyptian Day

23 December

The Secret of the Unhewn Stone/Last day of Saturnalia/Acca Larentis

This is the blank day of the Celtic tree calendar, the only day in the year not ruled by a tree and its corresponding ogham letter. Its name, the Secret of the Unhewn Stone, denotes the quality of potential in all things. As the Roman festival of Acca Larentis, today is sacred to the goddess Laurentina, mother of the Lares, an earth goddess who guards the dead and the seed corn. She commemorates the old year and the potential of the new.

24 December

Celtic tree month of Beth commences

The birch tree month, corresponding with the ogham letter Beth, is a time of purification and new beginnings.

25 December

Christmas Day/Goddess month of Astraea ends

The observance of Christmas contains many elements from a number of different religious sources. The many ceremonies and religious sources of the day make it the most important festival of the year.

26 December

Boxing Day/St. Stephen/Goddess month of Hestia commences

The custom of wren hunting was once widely observed on this day. The tiny bird, whose slaughter was prohibited at other times of the year, was imprisoned in a lantern or a wren house, then solemnly paraded around the village, hung on a holly branch and borne to its funeral by the "droluns" or wren boys.

27 December

St. John the Evangelist

A traditional feast day in freemasonry.

28 December

Bairns' Day/Holy Innocents' Day/Runic half-month of Eoh commences/ Egyptian Day

 Holy Innocents' Day, or Bairns' Day, commemorates Herod's slaughter of infant boys under the age of two. Folk tradition considers

Bairns' Day by far the unluckiest day of the year, when no work should be started. This is the month of rune Eoh, representing the dead, and the yew tree, sacred to winter shamanism.

29 December

30 December

31 December

New Year's Eve/Hogmanay/Asatru Twelfth Night

New Year's Eve/Hogmanay commemorates the solar divinity, Hogmagog. Traditional festivities include dressing in hides and horns of animals—"guising"—burning smoking sticks (Hogmanays) to ward off evil sprites, and eating special cakes. At the moment of the new year, doors are opened and utensils rattled to drive off the last psychic vestiges of the old year and welcome the new:

> *Get up, good wife, and shake your feathers,*
> *And dinna think that we are beggars;*
> *For we are bairns come out to play,*
> *Get up and gie' us our Hogmanay.*

appendix: charts

The following charts for the years 1993-2000 are for movable feasts (marked with a ☽ in the calendar) and the solstices and equinoxes (marked with a ☉ in the calendar). A month-by-month lunation table for all eight years is also included.

Movable Days ☽

	1993	1994	1995	1996	1997	1998	1999	2000
Disting Moon	Jan 8	Jan 27	Jan 16	Jan 5	Jan 23	Jan 12	Jan 2	Jan 21
Plough Monday	Jan 11	Jan 10	Jan 9	Jan 8	Jan 13	Jan 12	Jan 11	Jan 10
St. Distaff's Day	Jan 12	Jan 11	Jan 10	Jan 9	Jan 14	Jan 13	Jan 12	Jan 11
Purim	Mar 7	Feb 25	Mar 16	Mar 5	Mar 23	Mar 12	Mar 2	Mar 21
Passover	Apr 6	Mar 27	Apr 15	Apr 4	Apr 22	Apr 11	Apr 1	Apr 20
Easter	Apr 11	Apr 3	Apr 16	Apr 7	Mar 30	Apr 12	Apr 4	Apr 23
Enlightenment of the Buddha	May 6	May 25	May 14	May 3	May 22	May 11	May 30	May 18
Ascension/Mjollnir	May 20	May 12	May 25	May 16	May 8	May 21	May 13	June 1
Whitsunday	May 30	May 22	June 4	May 26	May 18	May 31	May 23	June 11
Mother Shipton's Day	June 2	May 25	June 7	May 29	May 21	June 3	May 26	June 14
Islamic New Year	June 21	June 10	May 31	May 19	May 9	Apr 28	Apr 17	Apr 6
Rosh Hashanah	Sept 16	Sept 6	Sept 25	Sept 14	Oct 2	Sept 21	Sept 11	Sept 30
Yom Kippur	Sept 25	Sept 15	Oct 4	Sept 23	Oct 11	Sept 30	Sept 20	Oct 9
Simhat Torah	Oct 8	Sept 28	Oct 17	Oct 6	Oct 24	Oct 13	Oct 3	Oct 22
Winter Saturday & Sunday	Oct 23 & 24	Oct 22 & 23	Oct 28 & 29	Oct 26 & 27	Oct 25 & 26	Oct 24 & 25	Oct 23 & 24	Oct 28 & 29
Hanukkah	Dec 9	Nov 28	Dec 18	Dec 6	Dec 24	Dec 14	Dec 4	Dec 22

All times in the following charts are Greenwich Mean Time and are given in the twenty-four-hour system (1:00 P.M. is 13:00, 8:15 P.M. is 20:15, etc.). For Eastern Standard Time subtract 5 hours; for Pacific Standard Time subtract 8 hours. If the Greenwich time listed is less than 5:00, then subtracting 5 hours, the actual date of the equinox or solstice will be a day sooner in Boston. For example, the autumnal equinox in 1993 occurs on September 23 at 12:23 A.M. (00:23) at Greenwich but on September 22 at 7:23 P.M. in the Eastern Time Zone.

Similarly the moon will enter its first quarter on 1 January 1993 at 3:38 A.M. at Greenwich, at 10:38 P.M. on 31 December 1992 in Boston and at 7:38 P.M. on 31 December in San Francisco. In short, any time before 5:00 A.M. (GMT) occurs on the previous day—5 hours earlier in Boston and 8 hours earlier in San Francisco.

To determine real local time where you are, consult an almanac for the time correction factor based on your latitude and longitude. Add 1 hour for Daylight Savings Time. (All data from *The American Ephemeris for the 20th Century* by Neil F. Michelsen; courtesy of Astro Communications Services, P.O. Box 34487, San Diego, CA 92163.)

Equinoxes and Solstices ☉

	VERNAL EQUINOX		SUMMER SOLSTICE		AUTUMNAL EQUINOX		WINTER SOLSTICE	
1993	Mar 20	14:41	June 21	9:00	Sept 23	00:23	Dec 21	20:26
1994	Mar 20	20:28	June 21	14:48	Sept 23	6:19	Dec 22	2:23
1995	Mar 20	2:15	June 21	20:34	Sept 23	12:13	Dec 22	8:17
1996	Mar 20	8:03	June 21	2:24	Sept 22	18:01	Dec 21	14:06
1997	Mar 20	13:15	June 21	8:20	Sept 22	23:56	Dec 21	20:08
1998	Mar 20	19:55	June 21	14:03	Sept 23	5:38	Dec 22	1:57
1999	Mar 21	1:46	June 21	19:49	Sept 23	11:32	Dec 22	7:44
2000	Mar 20	7:36	June 21	1:48	Sept 22	17:28	Dec 21	13:38

Lunar Phases Month by Month

● New Moon

☽ First Quarter

○ Full Moon

☾ Last Quarter

Key to Chart

DAY   HOUR:MIN. PHASE OF MOON

1   3:38   ☽

1993

JANUARY		FEBRUARY		MARCH		APRIL		MAY		JUNE	
1	3:38 ☽	6	23:55 ○	1	15:47 ☽	6	18:43 ○	6	3:34 ○	4	13:02 ○
8	12:37 ○	13	14:57 ☾	8	9:46 ○	13	19:39 ☾	13	12:20 ☾	12	5:36 ☾
15	4:01 ☾	21	13:05 ●	15	4:17 ☾	21	23:49 ●	21	14:07 ●	20	1:52 ●
22	18:27 ●			23	7:14 ●	29	12:40 ☽	28	18:21 ☽	26	22:43 ☽
30	23:20 ☽			31	4:10 ☽						

JULY		AUGUST		SEPTEMBER		OCTOBER		NOVEMBER		DECEMBER	
3	23:45 ○	2	12:10 ○	1	2:33 ○	8	19:35 ☾	7	6:36 ☾	6	15:49 ☾
11	22:49 ☾	10	15:19 ☾	9	6:26 ☾	15	11:36 ●	13	21:34 ●	13	9:27 ●
19	11:24 ●	17	19:28 ●	16	3:10 ●	22	8:52 ☽	21	2:03 ☽	20	22:26 ☽
26	3:25 ☽	24	9:57 ☽	22	19:32 ☽	30	12:38 ○	29	6:31 ○	28	23:05 ○
				30	18:54 ○						

1994

JANUARY		FEBRUARY		MARCH		APRIL		MAY		JUNE	
5	0:01 ☾	3	8:06 ☾	4	16:53 ☾	3	2:55 ☾	2	14:33 ☾	1	4:02 ☾
11	23:10 ●	10	14:30 ●	12	7:05 ●	11	0:17 ●	10	17:07 ●	9	8:26 ●
19	20:27 ☽	18	17:47 ☽	20	12:14 ☽	19	2:34 ☽	18	12:50 ☽	16	19:57 ☽
27	13:23 ○	26	1:15 ○	27	11:10 ○	25	19:45 ○	25	3:39 ○	23	11:33 ○
										30	19:31 ☾

JULY		AUGUST		SEPTEMBER		OCTOBER		NOVEMBER		DECEMBER	
8	21:37 ●	7	8:45 ●	5	18:33 ●	5	3:55 ●	3	13:35 ●	2	23:54 ●
16	1:12 ☽	14	5:57 ☽	12	11:34 ☽	11	19:17 ☽	10	6:14 ☽	9	21:06 ☽
22	20:16 ○	21	6:47 ○	19	20:01 ○	19	12:18 ○	18	6:57 ○	18	2:17 ○
30	12:40 ☾	29	6:41 ☾	28	0:23 ☾	27	16:44 ☾	26	7:04 ☾	26	19:06 ☾

1995

JANUARY		FEBRUARY		MARCH		APRIL		MAY		JUNE	
1	10:56 ●	7	12:54 ☽	1	11:48 ●	8	5:35 ☽	7	21:44 ☾	6	10:26 ☽
8	15:46 ☽	15	12:15 ○	9	10:14 ☽	15	12:08 ○	14	20:48 ○	13	4:04 ○
16	20:26 ○	22	13:04 ☾	17	1:26 ○	22	3:18 ☾	21	11:36 ☾	19	22:01 ☾
24	4:58 ☾			23	20:10 ☾	29	17:36 ●	29	9:27 ●	28	0:50 ●
30	22:48 ●			31	2:09 ●						

JULY		AUGUST		SEPTEMBER		OCTOBER		NOVEMBER		DECEMBER	
5	20:02 ☽	4	3:16 ☽	2	9:03 ☽	1	14:36 ☽	7	7:21 ○	7	1:27 ○
12	10:49 ○	10	18:16 ○	9	3:37 ○	8	15:52 ○	15	11:40 ☾	15	5:31 ☾
19	11:10 ☾	18	3:04 ☾	16	21:09 ☾	16	16:26 ☾	22	15:43 ●	22	2:22 ●
27	15:13 ●	26	4:31 ●	24	16:55 ●	24	4:36 ●	29	6:28 ☽	28	19:07 ☽
						30	21:17 ☽				

1996

JANUARY		FEBRUARY		MARCH		APRIL		MAY		JUNE	
5	20:51 ○	4	15:58 ○	5	9:23 ○	4	0:07 ○	3	11:48 ○	1	20:47 ○
13	20:45 ☾	12	8:37 ☾	12	17:15 ☾	10	23:36 ☾	10	5:04 ☾	8	11:06 ☾
20	12:51 ●	18	23:30 ●	19	10:45 ●	17	22:49 ●	17	11:46 ●	16	1:36 ●
27	11:14 ☽	26	5:52 ☽	27	1:31 ☽	25	20:40 ☽	25	14:13 ☽	24	5:23 ☽

JULY		AUGUST		SEPTEMBER		OCTOBER		NOVEMBER		DECEMBER	
1	3:58 ○	6	5:25 ☾	4	19:06 ☾	4	12:04 ☾	3	7:50 ☾	3	5:06 ☾
7	18:55 ☾	14	7:34 ●	12	23:07 ●	12	14:14 ●	11	4:16 ●	10	16:56 ●
15	16:15 ●	22	3:36 ☽	20	11:23 ☽	19	18:09 ☽	18	1:09 ☽	17	9:31 ☽
23	17:49 ☽	28	17:52 ○	27	2:51 ○	26	14:11 ○	25	4:10 ○	24	20:41 ○
30	10:35 ○										

1997

JANUARY		FEBRUARY		MARCH		APRIL		MAY		JUNE	
2	1:45 ☾	7	15:06 ●	2	9:38 ☾	7	11:02 ●	6	20:47 ●	5	7:04 ●
9	4:26 ●	14	8:58 ☽	9	1:15 ●	14	17:07 ☽	14	10:55 ☽	13	4:52 ☽
15	20:02 ☽	22	10:27 ○	16	0:06 ☽	22	20:34 ○	22	9:13 ○	20	19:09 ○
23	15:11 ○			24	4:45 ○	30	2:37 ☾	29	7:51 ☾	27	12:42 ☾
31	19:40 ☾			31	19:38 ☾						

JULY		AUGUST		SEPTEMBER		OCTOBER		NOVEMBER		DECEMBER	
4	18:40 ●	3	8:14 ●	1	23:52 ●	1	16:52 ●	7	21:43 ☽	7	6:09 ☽
12	21:44 ☽	11	12:42 ☽	10	1:31 ☽	9	12:22 ☽	14	14:12 ○	14	2:37 ○
20	3:20 ○	18	10:55 ○	16	18:51 ○	16	3:46 ○	21	23:58 ☾	21	21:43 ☾
26	18:28 ☾	25	2:24 ☾	23	13:35 ☾	23	4:48 ☾	30	2:14 ●	29	16:57 ●
						31	10:01 ●				

1998

JANUARY		FEBRUARY		MARCH		APRIL		MAY		JUNE	
5	14:18 ☽	3	22:53 ☽	5	8:41 ☽	3	20:18 ☽	3	10:04 ☽	2	1:45 ☽
12	17:24 ○	11	10:23 ○	13	4:34 ○	11	22:24 ○	11	14:29 ○	10	4:18 ○
20	19:40 ☾	19	15:27 ☾	21	7:38 ☾	19	19:53 ☾	19	4:35 ☾	17	10:38 ☾
28	6:01 ●	26	17:26 ●	28	3:14 ●	26	11:41 ●	25	19:32 ●	24	3:50 ●

JULY		AUGUST		SEPTEMBER		OCTOBER		NOVEMBER		DECEMBER	
1	18:43 ☽	8	2:10 ○	6	11:21 ○	5	20:12 ○	4	5:18 ○	3	15:19 ○
9	16:01 ○	14	19:49 ☾	13	1:58 ☾	12	11:11 ☾	11	0:28 ☾	10	17:54 ☾
16	15:13 ☾	22	2:03 ●	20	17:02 ●	20	10:09 ●	19	4:27 ●	18	22:42 ●
23	13:44 ●	30	5:07 ☽	28	21:11 ☽	28	11:46 ☽	27	0:23 ☽	26	10:46 ☽
31	12:05 ☽										

1999

JANUARY		FEBRUARY		MARCH		APRIL		MAY		JUNE	
2	2:50 ○	8	11:58 ☾	2	6:59 ○	9	2:51 ☾	8	17:29 ☾	7	4:20 ☾
9	14:22 ☾	16	6:39 ●	10	8:40 ☾	16	4:22 ●	15	12:05 ●	13	19:03 ●
17	15:46 ●	23	2:43 ☽	17	18:48 ●	22	19:02 ☽	22	5:34 ☽	20	18:13 ☽
24	19:15 ☽			24	10:18 ☽	30	14:55 ○	30	6:40 ○	28	21:38 ○
31	16:07 ○			31	22:49 ○						

JULY		AUGUST		SEPTEMBER		OCTOBER		NOVEMBER		DECEMBER	
6	11:57 ☾	4	17:27 ☾	2	22:17 ☾	2	4:02 ☾	8	3:53 ●	2	22:32 ●
13	2:24 ●	11	11:09 ●	9	22:02 ●	9	11:34 ●	16	9:03 ☽	9	0:50 ☽
20	9:09 ☽	19	1:47 ☽	17	20:06 ☽	17	15:00 ☽	23	7:04 ○	18	17:31 ○
28	11:25 ○	26	23:48 ○	25	10:51 ○	24	21:02 ○	29	23:19 ☾	26	14:04 ☾
						31	12:04 ☾				

2000

JANUARY		FEBRUARY		MARCH		APRIL		MAY		JUNE	
6	18:14 ●	5	13:03 ●	6	5:17 ●	4	18:12 ●	4	4:12 ●	2	12:14 ●
14	13:34 ☽	12	23:21 ☽	13	6:59 ☽	11	13:30 ☽	10	20:01 ☽	9	3:29 ☽
21	4:41 ○	19	16:27 ○	20	4:44 ○	18	17:42 ○	18	7:35 ○	16	22:27 ○
28	7:57 ☾	27	3:54 ☾	28	0:21 ☾	26	19:30 ☾	26	11:55 ☾	25	1:00 ☾

JULY		AUGUST		SEPTEMBER		OCTOBER		NOVEMBER		DECEMBER	
1	19:20 ●	7	1:02 ☽	5	16:27 ☽	5	10:59 ☽	4	7:27 ☽	4	3:55 ☽
8	12:53 ☽	15	5:13 ○	13	19:37 ○	13	8:53 ○	11	21:15 ○	11	9:03 ○
16	13:55 ○	22	18:51 ☾	21	1:28 ☾	20	7:59 ☾	18	15:25 ☾	18	0:41 ☾
24	11:02 ☾	29	10:19 ●	27	19:53 ●	27	7:58 ●	25	23:11 ●	25	17:22 ●
31	2:25 ●										

Index